workb[ook]

sounds good!

Junior Certificate Music

Edco · Mary McFadden · Katherine Kearns

Acknowledgments

The music in this book has been reproduced with the kind permission of publishers, agents and composers as follows:

Ode to Joy (Taken from *Recorder Duets from the Beginning, Book 1*). Music by Ludwig Van Beethoven. Arranged by John Pitts © Copyright 1996 Chester Music Limited. All Rights Reserved. International Copyright Secured; *Tallis' Canon*, reproduced by permission of Kevin Mayhew Limited; *Joy in the Morning* courtesy of Peter Nickol; *Abeeyo* from *Voiceworks 1* © Oxford University Press 2001. Reproduced by permission. All Rights Reserved; *Waltzing Matilda* (Taken from *Recorder from the Beginning - Around the World*). Music by Marie Cowan. Arranged by John Pitts © Copyright 2000 Chester Music Limited. All Rights Reserved. International Copyright Secured; *Glory, Glory, Hallelujah*, reproduced by permission of Kevin Mayhew Limited; *Eye Level* by Jack Trombey. Reproduced by permission of de Wolfe Limited; *Old Folks at Home* (Taken from *Play Easy Recorder, Volume 3*) Words and Music by Stephen Foster. Arranged by Jerry Lanning. © Copyright 2003 Chester Music Limited. All Rights Reserved. International Copyright Secured; *The Birdie Song*, reproduced by permission of Valentine Music Limited; *Nearer, My God, To Thee*, reproduced by permission of Kevin Mayhew Limited; *Silent Night* (Taken from *Play Easy Recorder, Volume 2*) Music by Franz Grüber. Words by Joseph Mohr. Arranged by Jerry Lanning © 2003 Chester Music Limited. All Rights Reserved. International Copyright Secured; *The Young Person's Guide to the Orchestra* (6-bar extract) © 1947 by Hawkes & Son (London) Ltd. Reproduced by permission of Boosey & Hawkes Music Publishers Ltd.; *The Lark in the Clear Air*, reproduced by permission of Neil Martin and the West Ocean String Quartet; *The Briar and the Rose*, reproduced by permission of Music Sales Limited; *Lord of the Dance* by Sydney Carter, reproduced by permission of Stainer & Bell Ltd, London, England. www.stainer.co.uk; *This Land is Your Land*, written by Woody Guthrie © 1956 & 1958 Ludlow Music Inc. assigned to TRO ESSEX MUSIC LTD. of Suite 2.07, Plaza 535 Kings Road, London SW10 0SZ. International Copyright Secured. All Rights Reserved. Used by permission; *I Wish I Knew How It Would Feel To Be Free*, Music by Billy Taylor, Words by Billy Taylor and Dick Dallas © 1964 Duane Music Inc. assigned to WESTMINISTER MUSIC LTD. of Suite 2.07, Plaza 535 Kings Road, London SW10 0SZ. International Copyright Secured. All Rights Reserved. Used by permission; *Calypso*, reproduced by permission of Jan Holdstock; *Turn the Glasses Over*, from *150 American Folk Songs* © Copyright 1974 by Boosey & Hawkes Inc. Reproduced by permission of Boosey & Hawkes Music Publishers Ltd.; *Little Donkey*, reproduced by permission of Warner/Chappell Music Limited; *Curly Locks*, reproduced from *The Usborne Nursery Rhyme Songbook* by Caroline Hooper, by permission of Usborne Publishing, 83-85 Saffron Hill, London EC1N 8RT, UK. Copyright © 1996 Usborne Publishing Ltd.; *I Had a Little Nut Tree*, reproduced from *The Usborne Nursery Rhyme Songbook* by Caroline Hooper, by permission of Usborne Publishing, 83-85 Saffron Hill, London EC1N 8RT, UK. Copyright © 1996 Usborne Publishing Ltd.; *Portsmouth*, reproduced from *Usborne Easy Recorder Tunes* by Anthony Marks, by permission of Usborne Publishing, 83-85 Saffron Hill, London EC1N 8RT, UK. Copyright © 2003 Usborne Publishing Ltd.; *Goosey, Goosey Gander*, reproduced from *The Usborne Nursery Rhyme Songbook* by Caroline Hooper, by permission of Usborne Publishing, 83-85 Saffron Hill, London EC1N 8RT, UK. Copyright © 1996 Usborne Publishing Ltd.; *The Knight's Song*, reproduced from *Usborne Easy Recorder Tunes* by Anthony Marks, by permission of Usborne Publishing, 83-85 Saffron Hill, London EC1N 8RT, UK. Copyright © 2003 Usborne Publishing Ltd.; *I am extremely musical, My voice is quite sublime*, reproduced by permission of Dr. Gervase Phinn; *I Wish I Were a Crotchet* by Roger McGough from *In the Glassroom* (© Roger McGough 1976) is printed by permission of United Agents (www.unitedagents.co.uk) on behalf of Roger McGough; *Sea Fever*, reproduced by permission of The Society of Authors as the Literary Representative of the Estate of John Masefield; *A Tiger in the Zoo* by Leslie Norris © Copyright Dr Meic Stephens; *Human Family* © Copyright 1990 by Maya Angelou. Reprinted by permission of The Helen Brann Agency, Inc.; The lines from *A Christmas Childhood* by Patrick Kavanagh are reprinted from *Collected Poems*, edited by Antoinette Quinn (Allen Lane, 2004), by kind permission of the Trustees of the Estate of the late Katherine B. Kavanagh, through the Jonathan Williams Literary Agency; *The Listeners*, reproduced by permission of The Trustees of Walter de la Mare and The Society of Authors as their representative; *The Lake Isle of Innisfree*, reproduced by permission of A P Watt Ltd. on behalf of Gráinne Yeats; *Na Coisithe*, reproduced by permission of An Gúm; *Le Linn ár nÓige*, reproduced by permission of Cló Iar-Chonnacht.

While every care has been taken to trace and acknowledge copyright, the publishers tender their apologies for any accidental infringement where copyright has proved untraceable. They would be pleased to come to a suitable arrangement with the rightful owner in each case.

All illustrations in this book are by Derry Dillon. Photographs are courtesy of the following: Shane McCarthy p.28, Acabella p.34, Alamy p.56, p.63, p.66, p.85, p.95, Wikipedia p48, Photocall Ireland p.57, Redferns p.72, p.90, p.94, Getty Images p.79, p.94, p.99, Frank Dolan p.94, Mary Bergin p.94, Roberta Cotter p.95. All other photos from Shutterstock and istockphoto.

CDs

Throughout this workbook you will find images of CDs, some of which refer back to the *Sounds Good! Core Book* and some to the *Sounds Good! Workbook*. These are colour coded to make it easier for students to identify them – so the Core Book CDs will be in yellow and orange and the Workbook CDs will be in blue and green like those below.

CDs are clearly labelled

Track numbers are indicated on the CDs

Foreword

This workbook integrates with and supports the *Sounds Good!* Core Book. It provides further information and resources for students and teachers, linking back to the recordings on the Core Book CDs, and includes a new CD with many original recordings.

The wealth of exercises included will help students to assimilate the concepts they have learnt in the core book and consolidate the information. There are crosswords, word searches and colourful illustrations that will appeal to visual learners and engage students who find text-based material more challenging. All aspects of the course are covered and dealt with in detail. There are listening questions for all of the choice songs and works in the core book.

New recordings of hornpipes, jigs, reels and slip jigs in the Irish music chapter will be a valuable resource for dance recognition and for students to play again and again to become familiar with the dances. The piece by the Chieftains in the Core Book is included on the workbook CD so that students can listen to it and answer the questions. Also a recording by Martin Hayes is included to introduce students to his magical style of playing the fiddle.

The recorded dictations will give students material to build up their dictation skills for a challenging aspect of the course. They can use these to become very familiar with the rhythms and pitches by clapping and singing them using solfa.

The composing chapters are now supported by many exercises that build up in difficulty from basic level to Junior Certificate standard. This will help the beginners in musical literacy to develop confidence in reading and writing music. There are many exam-type questions to provide resources for students and teachers to use from first to third year, before they begin to use the exam papers.

The final chapter will help students to develop a study plan and have an overview of the material they need to know when the Junior Certificate exam is approaching in third year.

Performing skills are also dealt with so that students can outline their repertoire choice and their rehearsal plans and get focused for their exam – this is a significant 25 per cent of the overall marks.

We hope above all that by learning composing, listening and performing skills students will come to enjoy music for the rest of their lives.

Mary McFadden and Katherine Kearns

About the Authors

Mary McFadden, a graduate of UCD, teaches music and choir at Loreto Secondary School, Balbriggan, Co. Dublin, and is PPMTA representative for the Dublin Branch. She is currently working on an MSc in Educational Training and Management (eLearning Strand) in DCU; her research interest is in the area of music education as an entitlement for all children. Mary is co-author of the Junior Certificate music textbook series, *Sounds Good!*

Katherine Kearns is a B. Mus. Ed. graduate of TCD and teaches music in Loreto Secondary School, Balbriggan, Co. Dublin. She promotes music for all students and accompanies choirs in school events and choral competitions.

Contents

Musical Features

Ode to Joy

Beethoven

Ode to Joy, by Beethoven, is the main theme from the last movement of his Ninth Symphony, the 'Choral', where voices are introduced. Here it is arranged for a recorder duet.

Let's figure out the musical features in this piece of music. On the next two pages we will consider different musical features, and mark some of them in the coloured boxes.

Melody

The top line of the recorder duet is the melody line.

1 Five melodic features are listed below. Find them in the melody and complete the appropriate box in the matching colour in the musical score.

Repeated notes	Step movement	Ascending melody	Small leap	Leap of a 6th

2 Another melodic feature is the range of a melody.

Find the lowest and highest notes in the melody and fill them in here.

This melody has a range of a _____

Rhythm

Insert the rhythmic features listed below in the appropriate boxes in the musical score.

Dotted rhythm

Crotchet movement

$\frac{4}{4}$ time signature

Dynamics — loud or soft

There are four melodic phrases in this melody. The dynamics of each phrase are described below. Insert the correct Italian words or symbols in the musical score.

Phrase 1 Soft

Phrase 2 Moderately soft   Getting softer   Soft

Phrase 3 Moderately loud Getting louder

Phrase 4 Loud   Getting softer Moderately loud

Tempo

The tempo or speed of this music is Allegretto. Write it in the correct place in the musical score.

Explain what Allegretto means. _____

Harmony

1 Is this tune: Major ☐ Minor ☐ ? The tonality of the music is M __ __ __ __ .

2 Look at the chord symbols and choose the correct statement below:

The chords are major. ☐

The chords are both major and minor. ☐

> In bars 11 and 12 the lower part in the recorder duet plays the note D in long notes. This is *soh* in tonic solfa, and also called the dominant note.
>
> Here it is a **dominant pedal**.

3 The two chords at the end of phrase 1 are ☐ and ☐ .

This is an unfinished cadence, called an I __ __ __ __ __ __ __ __ cadence.

4 The chords at the end of phrase 2 are: ☐ and ☐ .

This is a finished cadence, called a P __ __ __ __ __ __ cadence.

Texture

Choose the correct term to describe the texture of the music in this piece.

☐ Monophonic (single line melody)

☐ Homophonic (melody with harmonic accompaniment)

☐ Polyphonic (two or more melodies weaving together)

Form

Complete the boxes for the form on the musical score of this 4-phrase melody.

The form is [ ][ ][ ][ ]

Which word describes this form: Binary ☐   Rondo ☐   Ternary ☐

Tone Colour / Timbre

Describe the recorder sound:

Bright ☐   Deep ☐

Mood

What do you think is the mood of this piece?

Sad ☐   Joyful ☐   Dramatic ☐

Performing Medium

Ode to Joy has been arranged for:

Flute and piano ☐

Recorder duet ☐

Violin and piano ☐

Style

What is the style of *Ode to Joy*?

Jazz ☐

Classical ☐

Folk ☐

Complete the musical features below:

M _ _ _ _ _

R _ _ _ _ _

D _ _ _ _ _ _ _ _

F _ _ _

M _ _ _

Musical Features

S _ _ _ _

T _ _ _ _

H _ _ _ _ _ _

T _ _ _ _ _ _

T _ _ _ _ _ _

Wordsearch — Musical Features

L	S	B	A	R	J	G	D	B	M	J	J
L	D	B	Q	N	S	Y	N	S	R	X	N
R	P	C	E	X	N	T	F	R	T	U	H
M	H	G	I	A	M	I	Y	E	I	A	E
J	O	J	M	M	P	O	X	L	R	M	F
A	C	I	H	L	H	T	O	M	E	P	O
Z	C	I	J	B	U	T	O	D	F	L	R
S	Q	C	D	R	H	N	Y	P	W	F	M
Q	S	M	E	O	I	G	V	H	M	F	O
K	P	C	V	C	L	F	A	Z	R	E	Z
S	J	V	G	Q	U	E	Q	Y	X	W	T
R	E	N	O	Z	T	I	M	B	R	E	I

DYNAMICS   RHYTHMIC

FORM   STYLE

HARMONIC   TEMPO

MELODIC   TEXTURE

MOOD   TIMBRE

Crossword — Musical Features

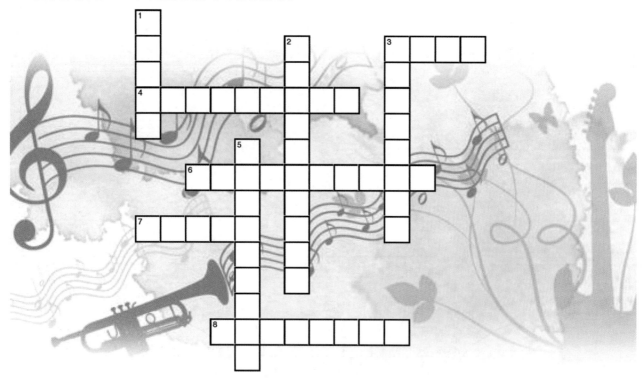

Across

3. When the melody moves up or down to the nearest note (4)

4. Moving in semitones (9)

6. When the melody goes down (10)

7. The distance from the lowest to the highest notes in the melody (5)

8. The distance between two notes (8)

Down

1. How high or low the notes are (5)

2. When the melody goes up or down eight notes (6, 4)

3. When the same musical idea is repeated higher or lower (8)

5. When the melody goes up (9)

Form

A basic unit of musical form is a P __ __ __ __ __ __ .

A melody with two different phrases, as follows: | A | B | is in B __ __ __ __ __ __ form.

The phrases may be repeated, so a melody with the structure below is still in _____ form.

| A | A | B | B |

A melody which has the first phrase returning after a contrasting phrase, as follows:

| A | B | A | is in T __ __ __ __ __ __ form.

Again, phrases may be repeated. This melody:

| A | A | B | B | A | is also in _____ form.

Texture

Here is a piece by Thomas Tallis, called *Tallis' Canon*. It can be played as a recorder duet.

Tallis' Canon

Thomas Tallis

Play each melody separately.

Then play both lines together, *but* begin at the same time. What do you discover?

_____

Now play the duet as it is written, with the second part starting a bar later than the first. What is the texture?

Monophonic ☐   Homophonic ☐   Polyphonic ☐

Explain why you chose your answer. _____

Joy in the Morning

Words by Kenneth Grahame
Music by Peter Nickol

Listen to the first two verses of 'Joy in the Morning' and follow the score, then answer the questions.

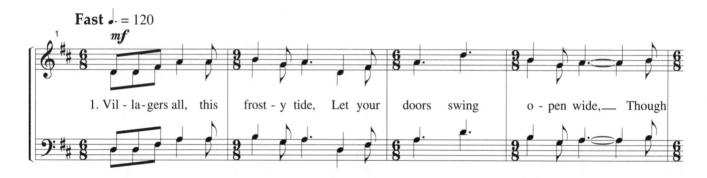

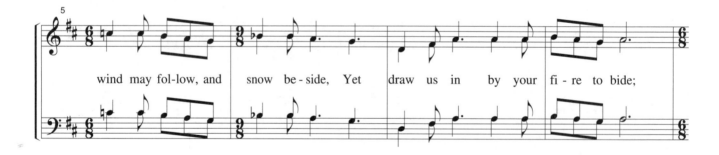

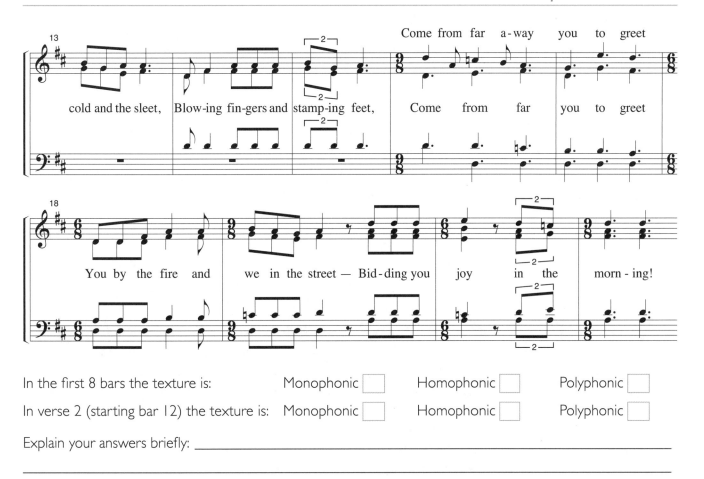

In the first 8 bars the texture is: Monophonic ☐ Homophonic ☐ Polyphonic ☐

In verse 2 (starting bar 12) the texture is: Monophonic ☐ Homophonic ☐ Polyphonic ☐

Explain your answers briefly: _____

_____

Abeeyo

Traditional Aboriginal

Now listen to the performance of 'Abeeyo', a traditional aboriginal call-and-response tune, look at the score and answer the questions.

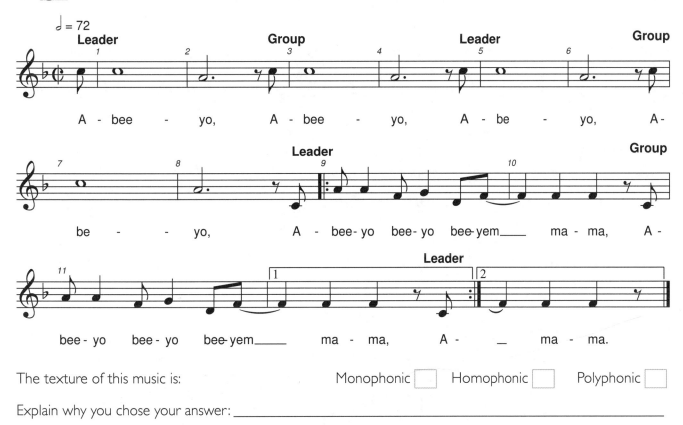

The texture of this music is: Monophonic ☐ Homophonic ☐ Polyphonic ☐

Explain why you chose your answer: _____

Meeting Musical Features in NEW TUNES!

The following musical pieces provide additional repertoire for recorder as well as providing further material for recognising musical features both visually and aurally (you can play and listen).

The first example, 'Waltzing Matilda', is completed so you can see how to approach this type of exercise, and there are more worked examples in the Core Book, pages 7–13.

Various musical features are colour-coded on the score. Name the feature and write it into the relevant box at the bottom of the page, with the correct bar number.

It is important to recognise them from looking at the score.

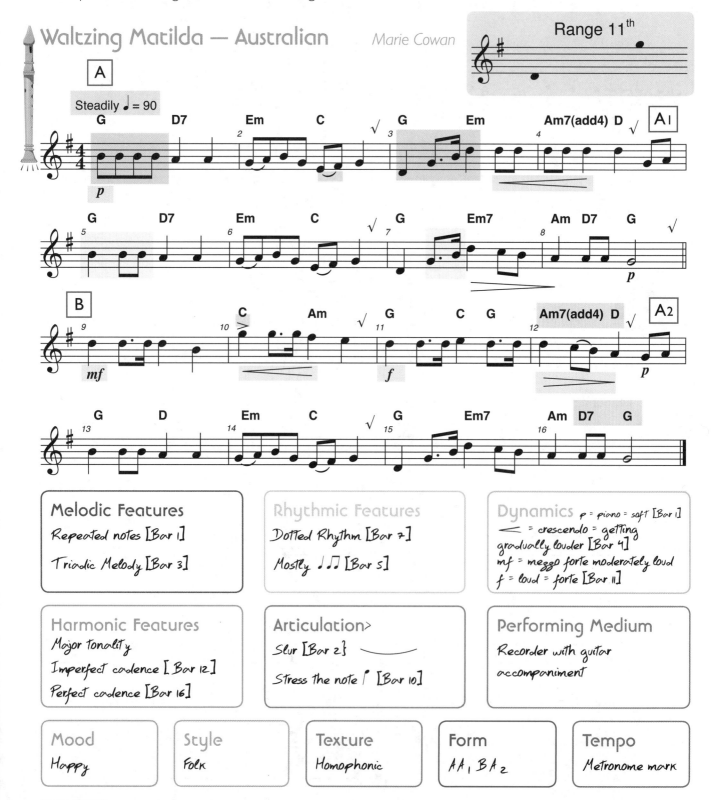

Melodic Features
Repeated notes [Bar 1]
Triadic Melody [Bar 3]

Rhythmic Features
Dotted Rhythm [Bar 7]
Mostly ♩♫ [Bar 5]

Dynamics p = piano = soft [Bar 1]
⟨ = crescendo = getting
gradually louder [Bar 4]
mf = mezzo forte moderately loud
f = loud = forte [Bar 11]

Harmonic Features
Major Tonality
Imperfect cadence [Bar 12]
Perfect cadence [Bar 16]

Articulation>
Slur [Bar 2]
Stress the note f [Bar 10]

Performing Medium
Recorder with guitar
accompaniment

Mood
Happy

Style
Folk

Texture
Homophonic

Form
AA₁ BA₂

Tempo
Metronome mark

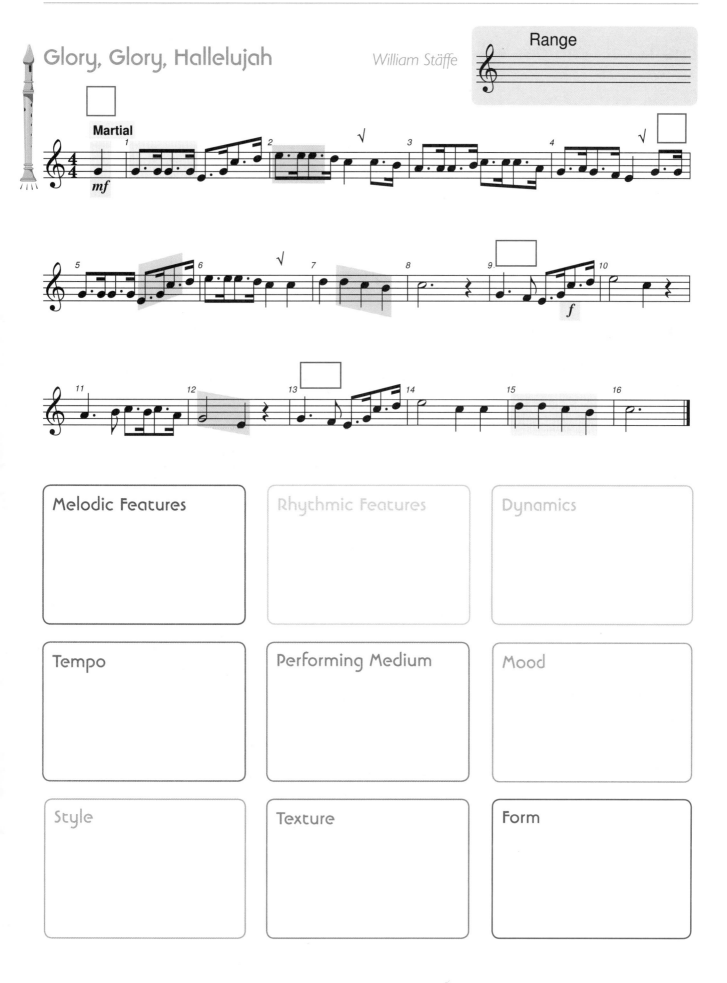

Glory, Glory, Hallelujah

William Stäffe

Range

Martial

Melodic Features

Rhythmic Features

Dynamics

Tempo

Performing Medium

Mood

Style

Texture

Form

Eye Level (Van der Valk Theme)   *Jack Trombey*

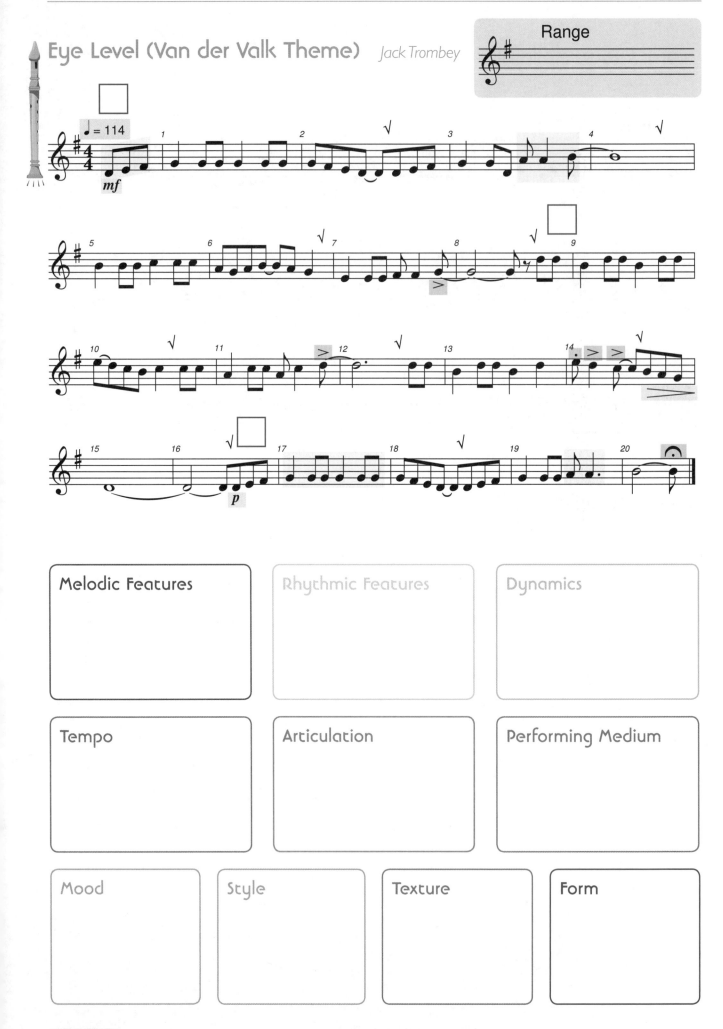

Melodic Features	Rhythmic Features	Dynamics

Tempo	Articulation	Performing Medium

Mood	Style	Texture	Form

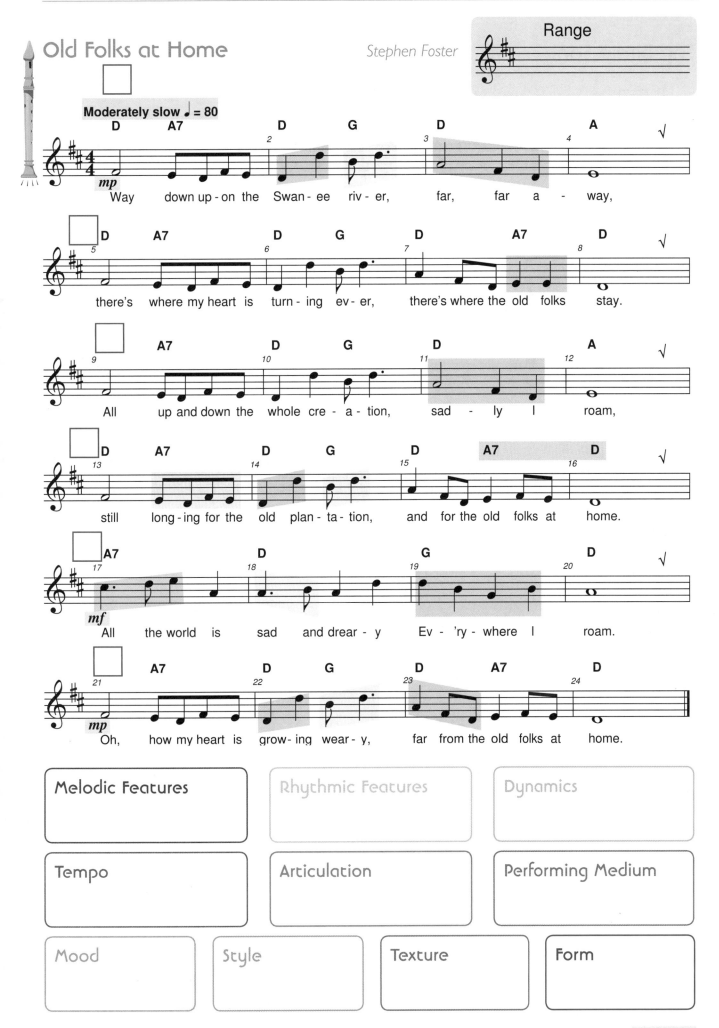

The Birdie Song

Terry Rendall/Werner Thomas

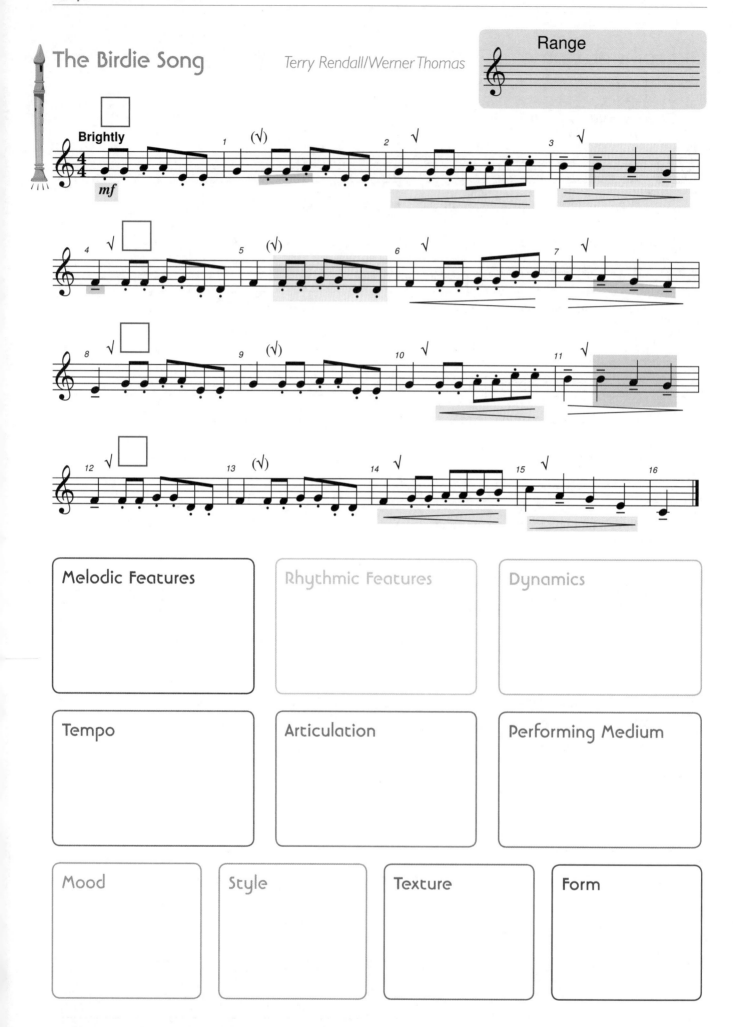

Melodic Features	Rhythmic Features	Dynamics

Tempo	Articulation	Performing Medium

Mood	Style	Texture	Form

Nearer, My God, To Thee

Lowell Mason

Melodic Features	Rhythmic Features	Dynamics

Tempo	Articulation	Performing Medium

Mood	Style	Texture	Form

Silent Night

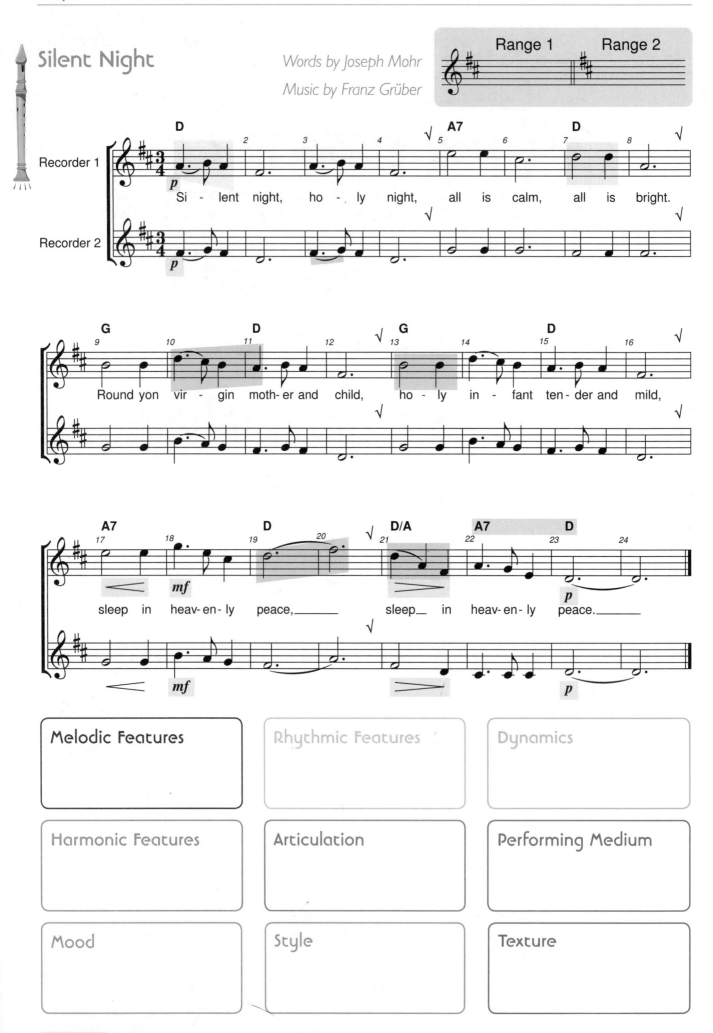

Words by Joseph Mohr

Music by Franz Grüber

Melodic Features

Rhythmic Features

Dynamics

Harmonic Features

Articulation

Performing Medium

Mood

Style

Texture

1. The Sections of the Orchestra

There are four main sections or families in the orchestra. Name four instruments belonging to each section in the table provided below.

Woodwind	Brass	Percussion	Strings

2. The Orchestra in Concert

Look at this picture of an orchestral concert. Label those involved, using the list provided.

audience	conductor	choir	orchestra	leader
composer (standing up in audience to receive applause)			flute soloist	

Research a famous orchestra or the Irish Youth Orchestra and write about what it is like to be in an orchestra from the point of view of a performer.

3. Orchestra Crossword

Across

1. large circular metal plate hit with a mallet (4)
4. woodwind instrument played by James Galway (5)
6. uses the alto clef (5)
7. brass instrument played with a slide (8)
9. shrill woodwind instrument (7)
10. tuned percussion instrument with set of wooden bars (9)
11. double-reed woodwind instrument played by David Agnew (4)
12. single reed woodwind instrument (8)
13. lowest instrument in string family (6, 4)
15. largest of brass family (4)
16. highest instrument of brass family (7)

Down

2. tuned percussion instrument with metal plates (12)
3. smallest instrument of string family (6)
4. played with hand held in bell (6, 4)
5. large woodwind instrument, plays bass line (7)
8. held between knees and stands on a spike (5)
14. type of side drum (5)

4. Orchestra Wordsearch

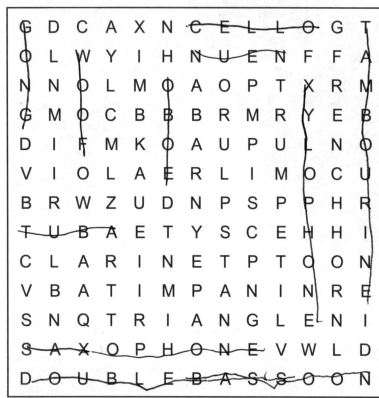

BASSOON
CELLO
CLARINET
CYMBALS
DOUBLE BASS
FRENCH HORN
GONG
OBOE
SNARE DRUM
TIMPANI
TROMBONE
TUBA
VIOLIN
XYLOPHONE
FLUTE
TRUMPET
TRIANGLE
GLOCKENSPIEL
HARP
TAMBOURINE
SAXOPHONE
VIOLA

5. Which Instrument Am I?

Now look at the instruments of the orchestra illustrated here and name each one, taking care to spell them correctly!

1. Flute
2. Small Flute
3. clarinet
4. clarinet
5. Harp
6. TRUMPet
7. trombone
8.
9.
10.
11.
12.
13.
14.
15.
16.
17.
18.
19.
20.
21.
22.
23.
24.
25.
26.
27.

6. Which Part Belongs to Which Instrument?

Match the correct part to each instrument. Be careful though: some parts fit with more than one instrument, but only one option has been assigned to each here. You may need to research this!

Jumbled here!		Rewrite correctly here!	
Instrument	Part	Instrument	Part
Violin	Double reed		
Cello	Head joint		
Flute	Two keyboards		
Oboe	Metal disc		
Clarinet	Folded tube		
Bassoon	Ivory keys		
Trombone	Mallet		
French horn	Valves		
Glockenspiel	Batter head		
Snare drum	Slide		
Cymbals	Peg		
Harpsichord	Spike		
Piano	Bell		

7. Famous Performers of Orchestral Instruments

Look at this crossword. The clues are famous performers of orchestral instruments. Fill in the instrument they play in the crossword. (Chapter 2 of the Core Book has all the answers!)

Across

5. Nigel Kennedy (6)

6. Louis Armstrong (7)

7. Bertram Turetzky (6, 4)

8. Barry Tuckwell (6, 4)

10. Emma Johnson (8)

11. David Agnew (4)

Down

1. George Chisholm (8)

2. Evelyn Glennie (9)

3. Lionel Tertis (5)

4. James Galway (5)

9. Yo Yo Ma (5)

8. The Key People Involved in an Orchestral Performance

Identify each picture, writing the correct letter in the box beside it.

A I decide on the interpretation of the music in the score: how loud or soft, how fast or slow the music is to be played, and so on. I have a baton and I don't actually play an instrument in the performance. Who am I?

Compase

B I work on musical manuscript and also on a computer, writing melodies and harmonies and producing a musical score for the orchestra to play. I add dynamics and tempo markings too. Who am I?

Pachist

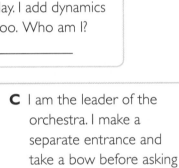

C I am the leader of the orchestra. I make a separate entrance and take a bow before asking the orchestra to tune up. What instrument do I play?

Violin

D I am the instrumentalist who, when the leader indicates to me, plays one single note, A, so that the orchestra can tune before we begin. What instrument do I play? Oboe

E I play the solo if there is a concerto in the concert. Who am I, and in this picture, which instrument am I playing?

double Bass

F I relax and enjoy listening to the beautiful music during the concert. I am one of the

audcince

9. The Conductor's Score

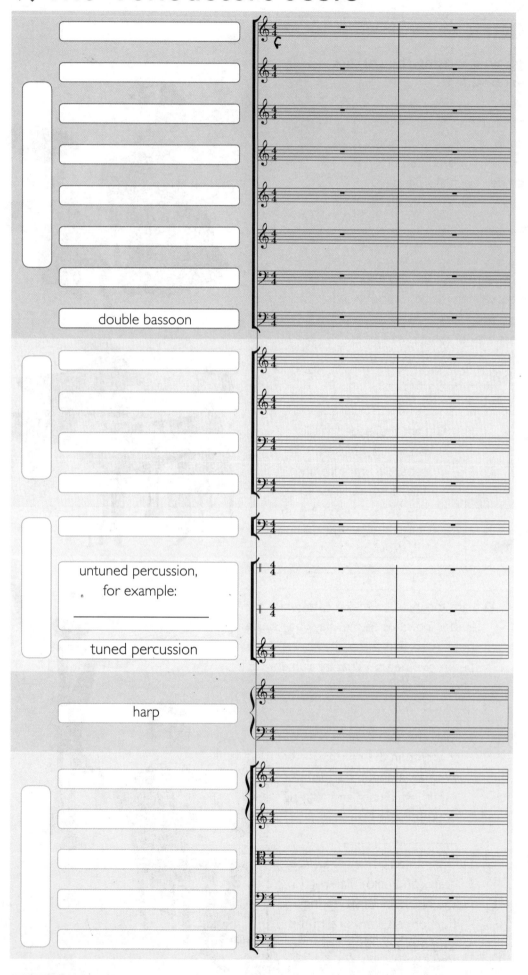

double bassoon

untuned percussion, for example:
_____

tuned percussion

harp

This is a blank conductor's score, with staves for all the main instruments of the orchestra. Fill in the **sections** along the left hand side first. Then add in the **names of all the instruments**. Try to do this from memory, but if you need to revise check out page 19 of the *Sounds Good!* Core Book.

Theme from *Schindler's List*

John Williams

(Core Book page 20)

Listen to the track, then choose the correct answers below:

1 This excerpt is:

dance music ☐   film music ✓   church music ☐

2 The **mood** of the music is:

Lively ☐   Sad ✓   Happy ☐

Can you suggest more words to describe the mood?

not very intresting ~~Rejected~~

3 The main theme is played by: ___ ? ___

Fill in the blanks below to complete the sentence:

4 The word **tempo** in music means the __ __ __ __ __ of the music.

5 The tempo of this music is

Allegro ☐   Andante ✓   Largo ☐

6 Explain in English the meaning of the Italian word you chose.

___ Piano ___ means ___ Soft enough and loud enough ___

7 The **dynamics** of a piece of music means how L o u d or S o f t the music is played or sung.

8 Choose from the bank of **dynamics** below and place them on the timeline.

Beginning   middle   end

♪ ♪

| forte   diminuendo   piano   crescendo |

9 Explain each of these dynamic markings:

(i) Forte _____

(ii) Diminuendo _____

(iii) Piano _____

(iv) Crescendo _____

Viola Concerto in G Major

Telemann

(Core Book page 21)

Listen to the track on the CD and answer the following questions.

1 The introduction is played by:

String family and harpsichord ☐   Woodwind family and harpsichord ☐

2 The melody line in the introduction is played by:

Violins ☐   Flutes ☐   Harpsichord ☐

3 The melodic line in the introduction features the following rhythm in some bars

This rhythm is: syncopated rhythm ☐   free rhythm ☐

4 The music begins on a: Downbeat ☐   Upbeat ☐

5 Another name for this is an A __ __ __ __ __ __ __ __ .

6 How many crotchet beats are there in every bar? _____

7 The tempo is P __ __ __ __ __ , which means _____ .

8 The solo instrument which enters is the V __ __ __ __ .

9 This instrument has a rich mellow tone. It is a member of the _____ family.

Viola players use a different clef from the treble clef or bass clef we are familiar with already. They read from an **alto** clef.

Here is the note **middle C** written in each of the three clefs:

Middle C   Middle C   Middle C

---

10 Choose the correct statement below:

When the solo instrument enters it plays:

The same melody as the introduction ☐   A new melody ☐

11 The solo instrument begins playing:

At the same pitch as the introduction ☐   An octave lower than the introduction ☐

12 Here are the first four bars of the piece.

s   d'   t   d'   t l s f m r   d   m   s   r'   m'   d'   r'

The following melodic features are included. Number them in the order they occur.

step movement ☐   scale movement ☐   upward leap ☐   triadic leaps ☐

13 Bar 2 features a major scale. Is it:

descending ☐   or ascending ☐ ?

Doce de Coco

(Core Book page 21)

Listen to the track on the CD and answer the following questions.

1 You hear a dialogue or conversation between the following two instruments:

Oboe and viola ☐   Cello and clarinet ☐

2 Which instrument plays the accompaniment? _____

3 What is the **mood** of the music? _____

4 What **style** of music is this?

Classical ☐   Jazz ☐   Popular ☐

Song of the Seashore

(Core Book pages 22 and 23)

Listen to the track on the CD and answer the following questions.

1 This excerpt of music begins with:

Plucked harp and shimmering (**tremolo**) strings ☐

Guitar chords and plucked (**pizzicato**) strings ☐

2 The instrument in the introduction plays:

Broken chords (**arpeggios**) ☐   Block chords ☐

3 The introduction also features:

Flute playing a **legato** (smooth) melody line ending on a trill ☐

Flute playing a **staccato** (short and detached) melody line ☐

4 The main melody is played by this instrument _____.

5 The accompaniment is played by _____.

6 Gradually the accompaniment is joined by _____.

Wind Quintet in A Minor, Variation 1

Reicha

(Core Book page 24)

Listen to the track on the CD and answer the following questions.

I Which solo instrument plays the busy quaver line of melody?

French horn ☐   Bassoon ☐   Clarinet ☐

2 The melody is played in the:

Low register ☐   High register ☐

3 Which of the following plays an accompaniment of sustained chords?

Woodwind ☐   Brass ☐   Organ ☐

4 Name any instrument you can hear in the accompaniment.

_____

5 The timbre (unique sound) of the solo instrument could be described as:

Deep and resonant ☐   High and bright ☐

Horn Concerto No. 4 in E flat

Mozart

(Core Book page 25)

Listen to the track on the CD and answer the following questions.

I Insert the time signature in the correct place on the score above.

2 The melody begins on an upbeat. This is also known as an A __ __ __ __ __ __ __ __ .

3 Copy the lowest note and the highest note you can discover onto the stave provided below.

4 The distance between these two notes is called the R __ __ __ __ of the melody.

5 The R __ __ __ __ of this excerpt is an interval of:

a 12th ☐ a 5th ☐ a 10th ☐

6 The excerpt begins with:

Solo horn ☐ Solo trumpet ☐

Overture to *Tannhäuser*   *Wagner*
(Core Book page 25)

Listen to the track on the CD and answer the following questions.

1 The main melody is played by:

Trumpet ☐ French horn ☐ Trombone ☐

2 The accompaniment is played mainly by:

Strings ☐ Woodwind ☐

3 Another family of the orchestra features later in the accompaniment:

Woodwind ☐ Brass ☐ Percussion ☐

4 Choose a word to describe the tempo.

Allegro (fast) ☐ Moderato (at a moderate speed) ☐ Adagio (slow) ☐

5 Describe the mood of the music: _____

_____

'Bydlo' from *Pictures at an Exhibition*   *Moussorgsky*
(Core Book page 26)

Listen to the track on the CD and answer the following questions.

1 What is the mood of the music in this excerpt?_____

_____

2 Which words best describe the accompaniment?

Plodding and repetitive ☐ Fast and lively ☐

3 What instrument is playing solo? _____

4 Name the family of the orchestra this instrument belongs to: _____

5 What is the tonality of the music?

Major ☐ Minor ☐

The Young Person's Guide to The Orchestra
Benjamin Britten

(Core Book pages 30–35)

Listen to the track on the CD and answer the following questions.

I This melody is in a minor key and begins on lah. Complete the tonic solfa under all the notes in the excerpt.

2 Look carefully at bars 3–6. What melodic feature can you find there? (See if there is a pattern.)

_____

3 Explain the characteristics of this feature in your own words.

_____

_____

4 At the beginning and end of this track we hear the full orchestra play together. Which Italian word means that **all** the players should play?

T _ _ _ _

5 After the opening statement, the four sections of the orchestra play separately, in turn. Name the sections, in the right order:

A [   ]

B [   ]

C [   ]

D [   ]

Chamber Music

1 The picture above illustrates chamber music. Explain why.

_____

_____

Crossword on Instrumental Ensembles

Across

2. A piece of music for seven instruments (6)

6. A small orchestra is a _ _ _ _ _ _ _ orchestra (7)

7. A piece of music for six instruments (6)

8. A piece of music for five instruments (7)

Down

1. A piece of music for nine instruments (5)

3. A musical group with piano, cello and violin (5, 4)

4. A piece of music for two instruments (4)

5. A piece of music for eight instruments (5)

The Lark in the Clear Air

Listen to the track on the CD, look at the printed music and answer the questions.

1 This folk song has been arranged for a string quartet. Complete the names of the four instruments:

1st V _ _ _ _ _

2nd V _ _ _ _ _

V _ _ _ _

C _ _ _ _

West Ocean String Quartet

© Shane McCarthy

Here is a score of the first verse (up to **01:02** on the recording):

ault.

2 The melody is passed from one instrument to another. Can you see on the score where this happens? Listen to the recording and follow the score. Using a coloured marker, highlight the melody line on the score. Fill in the instruments below when you have worked out which instruments play the melody in verse 1.

Bar 1–9 _____

Bar 10–13 _____

Bar 14–17 _____

3 The section from **2:03** to **2:37** sounds different. How would you describe the difference?

_____

_____

_____

4 Name two musical features in this piece and describe them below. For ideas of musical features, look back at chapter one.

  a) Musical feature: _____

     Description: _____

  b) Musical feature: _____

     Description: _____

Dona Nobis Pacem

Listen to the track on the CD and answer the questions.

I The solo instrument that begins is: Violin ☐   Cello ☐   Viola ☐

00:00–00:16

2 This section is:

Polyphonic texture ☐   Homophonic texture ☐   Monophonic texture ☐

3 Explain why: _____

_____

00:17

4 Name the second instrument that joins in: _____

5 This is a: trio ☐   duet ☐   quartet ☐

6 This section, from **00:17**, is:

Polyphonic texture ☐   Homophonic texture ☐   Monophonic texture ☐

7 Explain why: _____

_____

8 Name and describe two musical features of this piece that you like:

a) _____

b) _____

9 This music is played by a famous performer, Yo-Yo Ma. Find out about him on his website and write a note here. www.yo-yoma.com

_____

_____

_____

_____

_____

_____

4 | Voices

Registers

1 A voice has three main registers. Match each register with the correct range of notes.

Head Voice
Higher notes ☐
Medium-range notes ☐
Lower notes ☐

Chest Voice
Higher notes ☐
Medium-range notes ☐
Lower notes ☐

Middle Voice
Higher notes ☐
Medium-range notes ☐
Lower notes ☐

Soprano

Tenor

Voice-types

There are also different types of voice

Soprano	Bass	Tenor	Mezzo soprano	Contralto	Baritone

2 Which voice-type belongs with which of the ranges below?

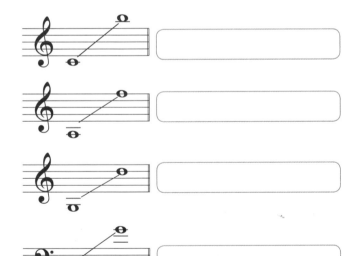

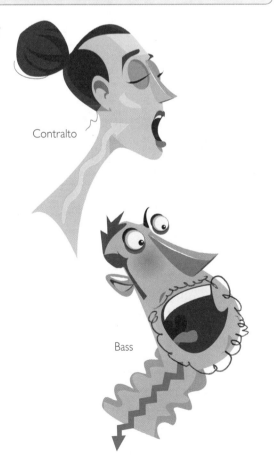

Contralto

Bass

3 Now complete the following table, writing in the voice-type again, but also finding the name of a well known singer for each type of voice.

High female voice		High male voice	
Voice-type:	Name of singer:	Voice-type:	Name of singer:

Medium female voice		Medium male voice	
Voice-type:	Name of singer:	Voice-type:	Name of singer:

Low female voice		Low male voice	
Voice-type:	Name of singer:	Voice-type:	Name of singer:

4 What is a treble voice? _a boys voice_

_____

5 Give an example of a well-known treble singer: _a boy_

'Evening Prayer' from *Hänsel and Gretel*   *Humperdinck*

Listen to this excerpt from 'Evening Prayer', arranged by Karl Jenkins and Philip Wilby.

1 The introduction is played by: Strings ☐   Guitar ☐   Brass ☐

2 The vocal group is a: Mixed Choir ☐   Female Choir ☐   Male Choir ☐

3 The vocal texture at first is: Homophonic ☐   Polyphonic ☐   Monophonic ☐

4 At **00:51** the texture changes to: Homophonic ☐   Polyphonic ☐   Monophonic ☐

5 Describe the mood of the music? _____

_____

Now is the Month of Maying

Listen to the track on the CD and answer the following questions.

1 This group is a: Male Choir ☐ Female Choir ☐ Mixed Choir ☐

2 The performance is unaccompanied (no instruments accompanying the singing).
Another word for unaccompanied choral singing is:

Acapella ☐ Solo ☐

3 Each verse has four phrases, with each phrase followed by fa-la-las. Listen carefully, then complete the
form in the boxes below, using the letters A and B:

4 The texture at the beginning is **homophonic**, a melody with chordal accompaniment from the other
singers. In the fa-la-las following the third phrase, at **00:22**, the texture changes. What is this type of
texture called?

_____

Kangivumanga

Joseph Shabalala

Listen to Kangivumanga, sung by Ladysmith Black Mambazo, a famous vocal group from
South Africa and answer the questions.

1 This song is in the form: Ternary ☐ Call and response ☐ Rondo ☐

2 What type of vocal group performs this song?

Mixed choir ☐ Male choir ☐ Children's choir ☐

3 Name a musical feature you hear in this music: _____

_____

The Briar and the Rose

Tom Waits

Listen to this song sung by the vocal group Acabella and answer the questions.

Here are the words of verse 1:

I fell asleep down by a stream

And there I had the strangest dream

'Twas down by Brennan's Glen there grows

The briar and the rose

1 Line 1 is sung by: Solo female voice ☐   Solo male voice ☐

2 The texture in line 1 is: Monophonic ☐   Polyphonic ☐   Homophonic ☐

3 What happens vocally in line 2? _____

_____

4 What happens in line 3? _____

_____

5 The vocal line *above* the melody in line 4 is called a: Harmony ☐   Descant ☐

Verse 2

There's a tree in the forest

And I don't know where

I built a nest out of your hair

And climbing up into the air

The briar and the rose

6 The **leap** in the melody on the underlined words
'There's a tree' is:

A third ☐   An octave ☐   A sixth ☐

7 This excerpt is unaccompanied choral singing.
What is another term/word for this?

_____

8 In the 4th line of verse 2, on the word 'air',
describe what the melody does here:

Acabella

© *Courtesy of Acabella*

_____

_____

9 Describe the mood of the song:

_____

10 Why do you think this group of singers is called Acabella?

_____

_____

11 What is a vocal group of five singers also called?

_____

Siúil a Rún

Listen to this excerpt from another performance by Acabella, this time of a traditional song. The lyrics are provided below.

Verse 1

I wish I was on yonder hill

'Tis there I'd sit and cry my fill

'Til every tear would turn a mill

Is go dté tú a mhuirnín slán

Verse 2

I will dye my petticoats, I'll dye them red

And round the world I'd beg my bread

Until my parents might wish me dead

Is go dté tú a mhúirnín slán

Chorus

Siúil, siúil, siúil a rún

Siúil go socair agus siúil go ciúin

Siúil go doras agus éalaigh liom

Is go dté tú a mhúirnín slán

Verse 3

I will sell my rod I'll sell my reel

I'll sell my own true spinning wheel

But to buy my love a sword of steel

Is go dté tú a mhúirnín slán

Chorus

1 This song begins with: Solo voice ☐   Piano introduction ☐

2 What is the texture of the first verse?   Monophonic ☐   Polyphonic ☐   Homophonic ☐

3 What typical Irish features can you hear in the singing?

_____

_____

4 This song is in two languages, Irish and English. What is another word for bilingual songs?

M __ __ __ __ __ __ __ __

5 What instrument joins in at the beginning of verse 2? _____

6 Describe the vocal texture in the choruses:_____

_____

7 What new instrument joins in the second line of verse 3?_____

8 This song is about a woman whose boyfriend is a soldier gone to war. What is the mood of the song?

_____

9 This Irish song is a: Dandling song ☐   Lament ☐   Drinking song ☐

10 What happens to the tempo/speed at the end of each verse or chorus? _____

_____

5 | Choice Works: Listening

There are six categories of 'choice works'. You will study at least one piece from each category, learning about its musical features and discerning the unique sound of the instruments. You must understand clearly why the piece you choose belongs to that category.

Dance Movements (see Core Book page 40)

These are usually composed to dance to. However, some dance music is composed for listening to only.

Functional dance music is composed for dancing, and usually has a suitable tempo for the type of dance.

Non-functional dance music has a dance rhythm but is composed for performance in a concert settting, not to accompany dancers. Therefore the music can be played at a slower speed.

Dances differ in the following features:

- how many beats they have in each bar
- the type of rhythms they use
- the tempo or speed

For example:

- A waltz has three crotchet beats in the bar, and usually a lively tempo.
- A gavotte has two minim beats in a bar, and is medium-tempo or quite lively.
- A sarabande has three beats in a bar and is slow and stately.

Can-Can from *Orpheus in the Underworld* *Offenbach*

(Core Book page 41)

Listen to the track on the CD and answer the questions.

1 This music belongs to the category:

Theme and Variations ☐   Film Music ☐   Dance Movements ☐

2 Give a reason why you decided it was in this category:

_____

00:00–00:12

3 The excerpt begins with an introduction. This features a dialogue between:

Strings and brass ☐   Woodwind and strings ☐

4 What percussion instrument comes in quietly during the introduction, at **00:06**?

Cymbals ☐   Tambourine ☐   Triangle ☐

00:12

Tune A

5 The tempo of the main melody at **00:12** is:

Allegro ☐   Andante ☐   Largo ☐

6 Explain the meaning of the tempo marking you chose:

_____ means _____

7 The first main tune (A) is mostly made up of which of the following types of notes?

♪♪♪♪ ☐   ♩ ☐   ♩ ☐   ♩ ☐

8 The tonality of the music is: major ☐   minor ☐

00:23

Tune B

9 The second tune (B) features four accented crotchets descending. Write an accent mark under the notes quoted below, and complete the sentence explaining what an accent does to a note.

An accented note should be played: _____

10 What dynamic marking would you suggest to the performer for this B phrase? Write it in the correct place on the musical score on the previous page.

11 At **00:29** the B phrase is repeated. What percussion instrument joins in loudly at **00:33**?

Triangle ☐   Gong ☐   Cymbals ☐

12 Describe how this instrument would be played by a percussionist and draw a rough sketch below of the instrument.

_____

_____

_____

_____

_____

_____

_____

00:39

Tune C

ff

13 The C theme comes next. This well-known melody is played by which family?

Percussion family ☐   String family ☐   Brass family ☐

14 The coda of a piece of music comes:

at the beginning ☐   at the end ☐   in the middle of the piece ☐

15 Which of the following is heard in the trombones very loudly (*ff*) near the end of the piece, at **01:50**?

Descending arpeggios ☐   Repeated notes ☐   Descending scales ☐

16 Describe the background to this famous piece from *Orpheus in the Underworld* by Offenbach, and highlight musical features that are memorable.

_____

_____

_____

_____

17 Name the piece and composer now, without checking anywhere else!

Name of piece: _____

Composer: _____

Dance of the Reed Flutes
from *The Nutcracker Suite*

Tchaikovsky

(Core Book page 42)

Listen to the track on the CD and look at the printed music, then answer the questions.

I The mood of the music is: Peaceful ☐ Lively ☐ Sombre (sad) ☐

2 The tempo is: Fast ☐ Slow ☐ Moderate ☐

00:00–00:05

3 The introduction begins with the lower strings playing: Pizzicato (plucked) ☐ Arco (bowed) ☐

00:06

4 The main melody is played by: Clarinets ☐ Flutes ☐

5 Choose the statement below that best describes the opening of the melody:

The opening of the melody features alternating notes ☐

The opening of the melody features an ascending scale ☐

6 A counter-melody is played in bar 19 **(00:38)** by another woodwind instrument with a rich deep tone. Which instrument?

Clarinet ☐   Cor Anglais ☐

7 In bar 25 the melody has some:

Chromatic (semitone) steps ascending ☐

Triadic (chordal) leaps descending ☐

8 In bar 25 the strings stop playing pizzicato. The Italian term marked in the score (in the string parts) is arco. Arco means:

To play with the bow ☐   To pluck the strings with the right-hand fingers ☐

9 In bar 43 a new section begins in the music (B). This melody is played by:

Oboes ☐   Clarinets ☐   Trumpets ☐

10 The melody here features: Leaps ☐   Scale movement ☐   Repeated notes ☐

11 Choose the statement that best describes the music of bar 51:

The violins repeat the music at the same pitch ☐

The violins repeat the theme an octave higher ☐

12 Choose the statement that describes the music at bar 60:

There is a rallentando and the music slows down ☐

There is an accelerando and the music speeds up ☐

13 Name the piece and composer now, without checking anywhere else!

Name of piece: _____

Composer: _____

Gavotte 1 from *Orchestral Suite No. 3 in D*   *Bach*
(Core Book page 44)

This music is from a Baroque suite. Listen to the track on the CD and answer the following questions.

1 Rearrange the jumbled words below to make a sentence to define or explain this type of suite.

> of   collection   suite   A   dances   a   contrasting   is
>
> _____

2 The tempo of the music is: Presto ☐   Andante ☐

3 Explain the meaning of the Italian tempo marking you chose:

_____ means _____

4 The time signature is $\frac{2}{2}$ This means we count:

Four crotchet beats in a bar ☐   Two minim beats in a bar ☐

5 What Italian phrase means $\frac{2}{2}$ time? Unjumble the letters below to make two words.

L A L A   V R B E E _____

00:00–00:14

6 The main A-section melody begins with: A step movement ☐   A small leap ☐   An octave leap ☐

7 The melody features: Ornamentation ☐   No ornamentation ☐

8 Choose the brass instrument that joins with the string family:

French Horn ☐   Trumpet ☐   Tuba ☐

9 Choose the keyboard instrument, common in the Baroque era, which is providing harmonic support here:

Harpsichord ☐   Piano ☐

00:30

10 The B section begins at **00:30** with: A downward octave leap ☐   Repeated notes ☐

11 Complete the form of the excerpt by filling in the letters in the boxes provided.

12 Explain how this dance belongs to the dance movements category, and highlight some memorable musical features.

_____

13 Name the piece and composer now, without checking anywhere else!

Name of piece: _____

Composer: _____

Symphonic Movements (see Core Book page 45)

Study page 45 of the Core Book before filling in the gaps in the following sentences:

A **symphony** is a p __ __ __ __ of music c __ __ __ __ __ __ __ for an o __ __ __ __ __ __ __ __ __.

Usually there are f __ __ __ sections called m __ __ __ __ __ __ __ __.

A common **musical structure** used in the symphony is s __ __ __ __ __ form.

This has three sections: E __ __ __ __ __ __ __ __ __ , D __ __ __ __ __ __ __ __ __ __ and

R __ __ __ __ __ __ __ __ __ __ __ __ __ .

A **symphonic suite** is a c __ __ __ __ __ __ __ __ __ of pieces which a composer may have

a __ __ __ __ __ __ __ from a previous work. If music from a b __ __ __ __ __ is arranged to perform in

a concert setting, it is called a b __ __ __ __ __ suite.

A symphony orchestra.

Symphony No. 9 ('From The New World') 2nd movement (Core Book page 46)

Dvořák

Listen to the track on the CD and answer the following questions.

1 The mood of the music is: Solemn ☐ Lively ☐ Playful ☐

2 The tempo of the music is: Allegro (fast) ☐ Largo (broadly) ☐ Andante (at a walking pace) ☐

3 The four-bar introduction is played by:

Brass and woodwind ☐ Woodwind and strings ☐ Brass and strings ☐

4 The changes in dynamic markings in this introduction could be described as:

pianissimo - - - - crescendo - - - - forte ☐ piano - - - - diminuendo - - - - pianissimo ☐

Now explain the choice you made, describing the dynamic change in your own words:

_____

_____

5 The introduction is mostly in:

semiquavers ♪♪♪♪ ☐ quavers ♪♪♪♪ ☐ minims ♩ ☐

6 The main theme is played by: Clarinet ☐ Flute ☐ Cor anglais ☐

7 This instrument is a member of the: Woodwind family ☐ Brass family ☐

8 Which of the following rhythmic features describes the main theme:

Smooth rhythm ☐ Dotted rhythm ☐

9 Fill in the form or structure of this short excerpt from the music:

A		

10 Explain why this piece belongs to the category Symphonic Movements, and highlight some memorable musical features:

_____

_____

_____

_____

_____

Dvořák

11 Name the piece and composer now, without checking anywhere else!

Name of piece: _____

Composer:_____

Eine Kleine Nachtmusik, 1st movement

Mozart

(Core Book page 50)

Listen to the track on the CD, look at the printed music on the page and answer the following questions.

1   The music in this excerpt is played by:

A full symphony orchestra ☐   A string orchestra ☐   A jazz band ☐

2   The music begins with all string instruments playing in: Octaves ☐   Harmony ☐

3   Choose a tempo marking from the list below, and insert it in the correct place on the musical score.

Largo (broad and slow) ☐   Allegro (fast) ☐   Andante (at a walking pace) ☐

4   This piece of music has one sharp in the key signature. It is in the key of _____

5   Insert the names of the instruments *in the correct place* at the beginning of the score.

6   Work out the tonic solfa (doh re mi, etc.) for the first 4 bars of the bass line. The scale is written here in the bass clef to help you. Write the solfa above the notes on the score.

7   Look at bars 6–15 of the score, and then at the following list of musical features. Find one example of each, somewhere in bars 6–15. Circle it on the score, and write the bar number in the box below:

Ornamentation ☐   Quaver rest ☐   A pair of semiquavers ☐

Two staccato notes ☐   Repeated notes ☐   Slurred minims ☐

8 In bars 18–19 the melodic line features: Arpeggios ☐   A sequence ☐   Repeated notes ☐

9 In bar 20 this instrumental technique 𝄽 on the violins is called:

Tremolando or tremolo ☐   Pizzicato ☐   Vibrato ☐

10 Bar 20 also features: Scale movement rising ☐   Triadic movement ☐

11 Which rhythmic feature appears in bar 24–25: Dotted rhythm ☐   Syncopated rhythm ☐

12 What new rhythmic feature appears in bar 28: _____

13 Look at bar 32 and describe:

Violin 1's music:_____

Violin 2's music: _____

14 The texture of the music here is:

Monophonic (single line melody) ☐

Homophonic (melody with chordal accompaniment) ☐

Polyphonic (independent lines weaving together) ☐

15 Draw a graphic illustration of the texture you have chosen in the box below:

┌──┐
│   │
│   │
│   │
│   │
│   │
└──┘

16 Explain why this piece belongs to this category, and highlight some memorable musical features:

_____

_____

_____

_____

17 Name the piece and composer now, without checking anywhere else.

Name of piece: _____

Composer:_____

┌───┐
│ This music is a **serenade** for strings, intended for outdoor │
│ entertainment in the evening. This is also known as chamber music, │
│ because it was composed for a small orchestra or ensemble. │
│   │
│ The **form** of the music is **sonata form**, with three sections: │
│ **exposition**, **development** and **recapitulation**. │
└───┘

Symphony No. 1, 3rd movement

Mahler

(Core Book page 51)

Listen to the track on the CD and answer the following questions.

Wood engraving after a drawing by Moritz von Schwind

Wikipedia

1 Which orchestral instrument plays the opening two bars?

Xylophone ☐   Timpani ☐   Bass drum ☐

2 This instrument is: Tuned percussion ☐   Untuned percussion ☐

3 Explain your choice of answer: _____

_____

4 This instrument continues with this same musical idea or pattern, repeated throughout the entire excerpt. This is called an O __ __ __ __ __ __ __ . This word comes from the Italian word meaning obstinate, to be fixed and determined.

> This movement is composed with a structure called a canon. The main tune is imitated several bars later by another instrument, and then another, and so on.

5 The first four instruments are listed below, but in the wrong order. Put them in the order in which they appear by numbering the boxes correctly.

Cello ☐   Double Bass ☐   Tuba ☐   Bassoon ☐

6 The tonality of the music is: Major ☐   Minor ☐

7 This is a well-known children's tune. Name it: _____

8 How is this version different from the original? _____

9 The mood of the music is: Joyful ☐   Peaceful ☐   Sad ☐

10 The fifth entry comes at **01:01**, when clarinet and bassoon join in with the first tune. However, at the same time something else happens, a different melody comes in as well. This is called:

A counter-melody ☐   A sequence ☐   An ostinato ☐

11 The solo instrument playing this new melody is: Flute ☐   Oboe ☐   Bassoon ☐

12 This piece is also programme music. This means it tells a story. Look at the illustration and describe the story.

_____

_____

_____

_____

13 Explain why this piece belongs to this category, and highlight some memorable musical features:

_____

_____

_____

_____

Theme and Variations (see Core Book page 54)

In **theme and variations form** the composer takes a theme or tune and presents it very simply at first. When the listener is familiar with the melody, it is presented again, changed and varied in interesting ways.

To learn about some of the ways in which a theme can be varied, read Core Book pages 54–55. This will help you with the following questions.

1 Give an example of a way the rhythm can be varied:

_____

2 Give an example of how the metre can be varied:

_____

3 Give an example of how the tonality can be varied:

_____

4 What other variations can a composer introduce to make the piece interesting?

_____

_____

_____

_____

Variations on Ah, vous dirai-je Maman

Mozart

(Core Book page 55)

Listen to the theme and variation tracks on the CD and answer the following questions.

The Theme

1 This piece is based on a familiar nursery song. What is it called?

_____

2 The tonality of the theme is: Major ☐   Minor ☐

3 Fill in the form of the theme in the boxes provided.

A			A		

4 The instrument playing the theme is: Xylophone ☐   Piano ☐   Harpsichord ☐

Variation 1

5 The right hand melody in the piano features:

Semiquaver notes, shorter and faster than the theme ☐   Steady crotchet notes ☐

Variation 2

6 This variation features:

Semiquaver notes in the accompaniment ☐   Semiquaver notes in the melody ☐

Variation 5

7 The rhythm of the original theme was simple crotchets

In this variation the rhythm is varied a lot. The new rhythm is:

☐

☐

☐

8 The mood of this variation is: Playful ☐   Dramatic ☐   Sad ☐

Variation 8

9 The tonality of this variation is: Minor ☐   Major ☐

10 Explain how this influences the mood of the music.

_____

_____

11 The music begins with this rhythm: ♩♩♩♩ . Which statement describes the beginning accurately?

Solo treble (right hand on the piano) plays an upward scale. ☐

Solo bass (left hand on the piano) plays an upward arpeggio. ☐

12 Almost immediately, at **00:03**, the other part enters:

Imitating the first part ☐   Playing repeated notes ☐   Playing block chords ☐

13 When the second melodic line enters it is played:

Above the opening melody ☐

At the same pitch as the opening melody ☐

Below the opening melody ☐

14 Explain how this music belongs to the category. Highlight some of the memorable musical features.

_____

_____

_____

String Quartet Opus 76 No. 3, 2nd movement   _Haydn_
(Core Book page 59)

Listen to the theme and variation tracks on the CD and answer the following questions.

1 This is a string quartet. List the four string instruments below, in order of highest to lowest range (or register).

_____

_____

_____

_____

The theme

2 The mood of the music is: Solemn and majestic ☐   Light-hearted ☐   Dance-like ☐

3 Which statement below best describes the music?

Single line of music ☐   Melody line with accompanying chords ☐

4 This texture is called: Polyphonic ☐   Monophonic ☐   Homophonic ☐

5 The tempo of the music is:

Allegro (fast) ☐   Poco adagio (quite slow) ☐   Andante (at a walking pace) ☐

6 Which instrument is playing the melody in the theme? _____

Variation 1

Listen carefully to the recording several times.

7 How many instruments play in this variation? two ☐   three ☐   four ☐

8 Which statement below best describes the music?

The melody of the theme is clearly heard, combined with a descant played in semiquavers ☐

The melody of the theme is varied a lot, with extra notes added ☐

9 The texture of this variation is:

Monophonic (single line of melody) ☐

Polyphonic (blending independent melody lines) ☐

Homophonic (melody with chordal accompaniment) ☐

> A **descant** is a harmonising line, usually played above the main melody.

Variation 2

This time listen very carefully to the melody line.

10 The melody of the theme is: Varied a lot ☐   Hardly varied at all ☐

11 Complete the following statement: The melody is played by an instrument with:

a bright high-register timbre ☐   a deep low-register timbre ☐

> **Timbre** is the unique sound of an instrument or voice. We recognise a person's voice even if we cannot see them when they speak. Likewise each instrument has its own unique colour and tone, which we get to know and recognise.

12 The accompaniment to the melody has two of the following features. Choose one from each type:

Rhythmic: Syncopation ☐   Minims ☐

Melodic: Scale movement ☐   Repeated staccato notes ☐

Variation 3

This variation features the viola playing the main theme.

13 The rhythm of the accompanying higher instruments is a:

Dotted rhythm ☐   Syncopated rhythm ☐

14 The texture is: Homophonic ☐   Polyphonic ☐   Monophonic ☐

15 When the cello enters in the lower register it plays:

Repeated notes ☐   Descending scale movement ☐   Ascending scale movement ☐

Variation 4

Look at the musical score of the first 8 bars of this variation and answer the following questions.

VAR. IV   A

16 Which instrument of the string family does not usually appear in a string quartet?

_____

Listen again to the theme track 23 and then to this variation track 27.

17 Describe what happens when the second phrase begins in variation 4, compared to the theme?

_____

_____

_____

18 The form of this variation is similar to the theme except there is some extra music added at the end to finish off the piece. The Italian word for this is c __ __ __ .

19 Three different clefs are used in this excerpt. Name each below and explain a little about them.

T __ __ __ __ __ clef _____

B __ __ __ clef _____

A __ __ __ clef _____

20 Explain how this music belongs to Theme and Variations category. Highlight memorable musical features.

_____

_____

_____

_____

21 Name the piece and composer now, without checking anywhere else.

Name of piece: _____

Composer: _____

West End Blues

performed by Louis Armstrong and the Hot Five

(Core Book pages 60–61)

Listen to the track on the CD and answer the following questions.

I Which style/genre of music best describes this piece of music? Classical ☐ Popular ☐ Jazz ☐

Introduction 00:00–00:12

2 The music begins with a solo played by: French horn ☐   Clarinet ☐   Trumpet ☐

3 This introduction has the following texture:

Homophonic ☐

Polyphonic ☐

Monophonic ☐

Chorus I   00:16–00:50

4 The melody is played here by the

_____

5 Choose the rhythmic feature you hear in the melodic line:

Strict rhythm ☐   Loose, syncopated rhythm ☐

6 Which term best describes the accompaniment?

Block chords ☐   Arpeggios ☐   Syncopated chords ☐

Chorus 2   00:50–01:23

7 The trombone plays the solo melody line here. An unusual percussive sound is heard. It is the syncopated sound of the:

Spoons ☐   Milk bottle ☐   Saucepan lids ☐

Chorus 3   01:24–1:59

8 The low register of the clarinet plays a variation on the melody here. Above the clarinet line the:

Singer improvises vocally using nonsense words 'wa wa wa' ☐

Trumpet plays a new melody ☐

Chorus 4   02:00–2:32

9 This solo variation is played by: Organ ☐   Piano ☐   Harpsichord ☐

10 The note values can be described as: Long held notes ☐   Short notes ☐

Chorus 5 (first part)   02:33–02:56

11 The instrument playing the melody here is the: _____

12 The two accompanying instruments playing crotchet chords are: P__ __ __ __ and B __ __ __ __

13 What is striking about the first phrase played by the soloist?_____

_____

14 Describe what happens to the tempo near the end of the piece, at **3:06**: _____

_____

15 Unjumble the Italian word for this tempo feature: **t a o r n a e n l l d**

__ __ __ __ __ __ __ __ __ __ __

16 What is scat singing, found in jazz music? _____

_____

17 In what way does this music belong to the category Theme and Variations? Highlight memorable musical features.

_____

_____

_____

_____

18 Name the piece and the main performer now, without checking anywhere else.

Name of piece: _____

Main performer: _____

Orchestrally Accompanied Instrumental or Vocal Music (see Core Book page 62)

Clarinet Concerto, 2nd movement

Mozart

(Core Book page 62)

Listen to the track on the CD and answer the following questions.

1 This excerpt is in: Classical style ☐   Popular style ☐   Jazz style ☐

> This music is from a **concerto**. A solo concerto is a piece of music where a solo instrument is accompanied by an orchestra.

2 The solo instrument playing the melody is: Flute ☐   Clarinet ☐   Oboe ☐

3 Which family of instruments accompanies the solo instrument at the start of this movement?
Brass family ☐   String family ☐

4 The tempo of the music is: Andante (walking pace) ☐   Allegro (fast) ☐   Adagio (slow) ☐

5 The mood of the music is: Peaceful and serene ☐   Lively ☐   Agitated ☐

6 The tonality of the music is: Major ☐   Minor ☐

02: 33–4:07

7 Listen to the second section of the movement, starting at **02:33.** Which of the following features does the soloist have?

Chromatic steps ☐   Descending arpeggios ☐   Leaps of more than two octaves ☐

Scale movement ☐   A trill ☐

8 Have you ticked them all? Well done! Look at the score on page 62 of the Core Book, and listen to the music again, following the score and identifying all the features listed above.

9 Explain why this music belongs to the category Orchestrally Accompanied Instrumental or Vocal Music. Highlight memorable musical features.

_____

_____

_____

_____

10 Name the piece and composer now, without checking anywhere else.

Name of piece: _____

Composer: _____

© Payless Images, Inc./Alamy

The Hallelujah Chorus from *Messiah*   *Handel*

(Core Book pages 63–64)

This piece is composed for a mixed chorus accompanied by orchestra. Listen to the track on the CD and answer the following questions.

Proinnsías Ó Duinn conducts Our Lady's Choral Society on Fishamble Street in Temple Bar at the opening of the annual anniversary performance of Handel's *Messiah*, part of the 2008 Handel festival.

I The four groups of voices in the chorus are:

> Bass   Alto   Soprano   Tenor

Write them in the correct place on the score below, to the left of the staves.

2 The tonality of the music is: Major ☐   Minor ☐

3 The key of the music is: F Major ☐   G Major ☐   D Major ☐

4 How many beats are there in each bar? _____

5 The orchestral introduction is: Two bars long ☐   Three bars long ☐   Four bars long ☐

6 The musical texture of the first phrase sung by the chorus is:

Polyphonic (independent melodies blending together) ☐

Homophonic (melody accompanied by chordal support) ☐

Monophonic (single line of melody) ☐

Listen to the first part of the Hallelujah Chorus, from the beginning up to **00:54**, and follow the words below. The lines of text are numbered to help you answer the next group of questions.

Line 1, 00:07	*Hallelujah, hallelujah, hallelujah, hallelujah, hallelujah*
Line 2, 00:16	*Hallelujah, hallelujah, hallelujah, hallelujah, hallelujah*
Line 3, 00:25	*For the Lord God omnipotent reigneth*
Line 4, 00:32	*Hallelujah, hallelujah, hallelujah, hallelujah*
Line 5, 00:37	*For the Lord God omnipotent reigneth*
Line 6, 00:43	*Hallelujah, hallelujah, hallelujah, hallelujah*
Line 7, 00:48	*For the Lord God omnipotent reigneth*

7 Underline the words where all the voices begin singing in unison or octaves.

> When a group of voices or instruments play or sing the same melody, the same notes, they are in unison. If they play or sing the same notes but an octave apart, they are in octaves. The effect is quite similar.

8 Which brass instrument plays loudly during the 4th line?

Tuba ☐   French horn ☐   Trumpet ☐

9 In line 5 the voices sing the same melody as line 3 but:

Beginning at the same pitch ☐   Beginning at a higher pitch ☐   Beginning at a lower pitch ☐

10 The words 'God omnipotent' feature:

A leap of an octave ascending then descending ☐

A leap of an octave descending then ascending ☐

11 The texture of the section starting at **00:48** is: Homophonic ☐   Monophonic ☐   Polyphonic ☐

12 Give a reason for your choice: _____

_____

13 This music is from an oratorio. Explain what an oratorio is, making statements about performers, text and subject matter, typical sections or movements:

Performers: _____

_____

Text and subject matter: _____

_____

Typical sections or movements: _____

_____

All the questions were about the first section of the Hallelujah Chorus. Now sit back and enjoy the rest!

Illustrative and Film Music (see Core Book page 65)

Theme Music from *Batman*

Danny Elfman

(Core Book page 65)

Listen to the track on the CD and answer the following questions.

1 The music begins:

With deep low-register notes played by woodwind and brass ☐

With bright high-register notes played by woodwind and brass ☐

2 The tempo of the music during the first section is: Lento ☐   Allegro ☐   Presto ☐

3 Explain the meaning of the word you selected:

_____ means _____

4 Dynamics in music describes:

The pitch of the notes: how high or low ☐   The loudness or softness of the music ☐

5 The opening bars of the music begin as follows: (Explain **both** answers, then select one.)

p ◁———— Explanation: _____ ☐

f ————▷ Explanation: _____ ☐

6 Which percussion instrument plays a 4-note descending motif at **00:20**?

Xylophone ☐   Glockenspiel ☐   Tubular Bells ☐

7 This musical motif is repeated several times. When a motif is repeated like this it is called:

A reprise ☐   An ostinato ☐   A ritornello ☐

8 The music gradually builds up and, between **00:50** and **01:05**:

Slows down ☐   Speeds up ☐

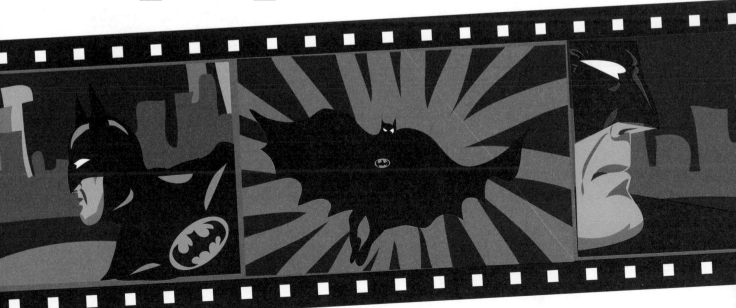

9 Listen to the entire excerpt. What do you think the composer is describing in the music?

_____

_____

10 How does the composer create a dramatic effect in the music? Mention musical features, dynamics, tonality and instruments in your answer.

_____

_____

_____

_____

11 Explain why this music belongs to the category Illustrative and Film Music. Highlight memorable musical features.

_____

_____

_____

12 Name the piece and composer now, without checking anywhere else.

Name of piece: _____

Composer:_____

The Elephant from _The Carnival of the Animals_ _Saint-Saëns_
(Core Book page 67)

Listen to the track on the CD and answer the following questions.

1 The two instruments playing in this excerpt are:

Piano and cello ☐

Piano and double bass ☐

Organ and tuba ☐

2 The melody is played by _____

3 The accompaniment is played by _____

4 The tempo is: Largo ☐   Allegretto ☐   Presto ☐

5 The tonality of the music is: Minor ☐   Major ☐   Atonal ☐

6 The mood of the music is: Sad and solemn ☐   Lighthearted and playful ☐

7 The music has the rhythm of a popular dance: Reel ☐   Jig ☐   Waltz ☐

8 The dynamics at the beginning are: Piano ☐   Forte ☐

9 Explain the meaning of the word you selected.

_____ means _____

The melody starts at bar 5. Here it is, from bar 5 to bar 12:

10 Now look at the musical features in the box below. Each of them can be found in bars 5–12. Enter them in the right place in the list below the box.

> Leap of a 4ᵗʰ   Leap of a 3ʳᵈ   descending scale movement   Leap of a 5ᵗʰ
>
> Sequence   Ascending scale movement   Step movement

Bar 5 ___Leap of a 4th_____

Bar 6 _____

Bar 7 _____

Bar 8 _____

Bars 9–10 _____

Bar 11 _____

Bar 12 _____

11 Describe how the piano accompaniment changes in the last section of the excerpt, at **01:07**.

_____

_____

12 How does the composer get the idea of 'elephant' across to the listener?

_____

_____

13 This music is programme music. What does that mean?

_____

_____

_____

14 Explain how this music belongs to the category Illustrative and Film Music. Highlight memorable musical features.

_____

_____

_____

15 Name the piece and composer now, without checking anywhere else.

Name of piece: _____

Composer: _____

Tortoises from *The Carnival of the Animals*   *Saint-Saëns*

(Core Book page 68)

Listen to the track on the CD and answer the following questions.

1 The music begins with:

Repeated chords played on the piano ☐

Repeated chords on organ ☐

2 The tempo is:

Very slow and mournful ☐

At a walking pace and majestic ☐

Fast and ceremonial ☐

3 The theme enters played by:

Woodwind family ☐   Brass family ☐   String family ☐

4 The mood is: _____

Listen to Core Book CD 1 track 13 (Can-Can) and then to this track 33 again.

5 Compare the two excerpts in the columns below.

	Can-Can	Tortoises
Melodic features		
Tempo		
Mood		
Instruments		

6 Explain why Tortoises from *The Carnival of the Animals* belongs to the category Illustrative and Film Music. Highlight memorable musical features.

_____

_____

_____

_____

Theme Music from
The Good, the Bad and the Ugly

Ennio Morricone

(Core Book page 69) Listen to the track on the CD and answer the questions.

1 Which of these three rhythms is played by timpani and bass guitar at the start of the excerpt?

2 The rhythm is repeated and continuous. This is called:

A canon ☐   An ostinato ☐   A sequence ☐

3 In the opening A section the structure is: Verse and chorus ☐   Call and response ☐

4 Another rhythmic idea is introduced at **00:24** by: Gong ☐   Bass drum ☐   Snare drum ☐

5 This piece was composed for which genre of film?

Horror film ☐   War film ☐   Western film ☐

6 Listen to the full excerpt and explain how the music helps to create the right atmosphere for this type of film, referring to musical features such as instruments, rhythms, mood, tonality, tempo:

_____

_____

_____

_____

_____

7 Name the piece and composer now, without checking anywhere else.

Name of piece: _____

Composer: _____

Concert Overtures, or Preludes or Intermezzi from Stage Works (see Core Book page 70)

Overture: *The Light Cavalry*

Suppé

(Core Book page 71) The recording is just one section of this overture.

Listen to the track on the CD and answer the following questions.

1 Ten musical features are listed below. Tick the six features that you can hear in this excerpt.

Repeated notes ☐   Trumpets in 3rds ☐

Clashing cymbals ☐   March tune ☐

Xylophone ☐   Waltz ☐

Accented notes ☐   Cello solo ☐

Varying dynamics ☐   Pianissimo throughout ☐

2 This is in ⁶⁄₈ time, with two strong dotted-crotchet pulses in each bar. Insert the time signature in the correct place in the score above. This time signature is an example of:

Compound Time ☐   Simple Time ☐

3 Explain why this music belongs to this category. Highlight memorable musical features.

_____

_____

_____

Prelude to *Carmen*

Bizet

(Core Book page 72)

Listen to the track on the CD and answer the following questions.

Section A   00:00–00:29

1 The tempo of the music is: Adagio ☐   Vivace ☐   Andante ☐

2 The tonality of the music is: Major ☐   Minor ☐

3 The full orchestra plays the melody. What is the Italian word for that? T __ __ __ __.

4 Name two percussion instruments you can hear in this excerpt.

_____ and _____

Section B 00:29–00:47

5 A contrasting melody is now played by: Violins ☐   Flutes ☐   Cellos ☐

6 The dynamics are now: Softer ☐   Much Louder ☐   Unchanged ☐

Section A returns – 00:47–01:02

Section C 01:02–01:29

7 The music in this section is an example of a: Jig ☐   March ☐   Fanfare ☐   Waltz ☐

8 The melody is played by: Violins ☐   Trumpets ☐   Cellos ☐

9 The accompaniment is played by: Woodwind ☐   Brass ☐   Percussion ☐

Listen to the music played on the violins.

10 At **01:27–01:29** there is a short joining-up bar. Listen to the violins here. They play:

A descending scale ☐   An ascending scale ☐   Repeated notes ☐

Section C repeats 01:29–01:50

11 At **1:29** the C section is repeated. Which statement is correct?

The repeat of C is played at the same pitch ☐

The repeat of C is played an octave lower ☐

The repeat of C is played an octave higher ☐

Last section 01:50–02:08

12 Describe the ending section of the piece. Do you recognise the tune from earlier?

_____

_____

_____

_____

_____

_____

13 Explain why this music belongs to this category. Highlight memorable musical features.

_____

_____

_____

_____

Intermezzo from *Cavalleria Rusticana*

Mascagni

(Core Book page 73)

Listen to the track on the CD and answer the following questions.

Section A 00:00–00:55

1 The melody in the opening bar moves upwards: doh – mi – soh. This type of movement is:

Triadic movement ☐

Step movement ☐

Scale movement ☐

Bridge 00:56–01:12

2 What instruments play the opening melody?

Violins ☐   Flutes ☐   Trumpets ☐

3 These instruments are playing:

Bright high-register notes ☐   Dark low-register notes ☐

Welsh National Opera Performing Cavalleria Rusticana in Wales Millennium Centre, Cardiff Bay, South Wales.

Bridge section 00:55–01:32

4 At the beginning of the bridge section, from **00:55** to **01:12**, there is a short dialogue or conversation between:

Strings and bassoon ☐   Strings and flute ☐   Strings and Oboe ☐

5 This piece ends with a coda. Explain what a coda is: _____

_____

_____

6 Explain why this music belongs to this category. Highlight memorable musical features.

_____

_____

_____

_____

_____

7 Name the piece and composer now, without checking anywhere else.

Name of piece: _____

Composer: _____

© The Photo Library Wales/Alamy

6 | Chosen General Study

- You must choose *one* topic that fits into one of the five categories below. For some ideas, look at page 74 of the Core Book, which lists some possible topics within each of the categories.

- When you have decided on a category and a topic, then assemble several pieces of music that fit into your topic, and learn as much as you can about them.

- Your general study is a project that you can enjoy, putting the skills into practice that you have learnt when studying songs and pieces. With your teacher guiding you, become an expert on your topic and know the background and the musical features.

Here are some suggestions to guide your research and listening. Complete your answers to the questions below when you have made sufficient progress, coming back to them later if necessary.

Choose your topic category from this list:

Day-to-day Music	☐	**Medieval and Renaissance Music**	☐
Ethnic Music from Other Cultures	☐	**Art Music in Modern Times**	☐
Popular Music and Jazz	☐		

Date: _____

My Chosen General Study is: _____

What CD recordings have you collected to research this topic?

(Try to choose really interesting contrasting pieces of music which you enjoy and will give you lots of scope to describe musical features).

_____

_____

How does your chosen music fit into this category?

_____

_____

Have you been to a performance? Describe what it was like if you have:

_____

_____

Choose two pieces of music you plan to study for this project. Make sure they are contrasting and have interesting musical features you can discuss and explain.

Piece of Music 1 _____

Piece of Music 2 _____

Who is/are the performer(s)? List their name(s) below.

_____

_____

_____

Who is/are the composer(s)?

_____

_____

What instruments are involved in the performances? List the names below.

_____

_____

_____

For each piece, find out about the background to the music, the composer, the performers. What was the inspiration behind the music? Focus especially on the musical influences.

_____

_____

_____

When you begin to listen and work out musical features, discuss with others and check with your teacher that you are focusing on the most important features. If you met someone who was 7 ft tall and were asked to describe their most distinguishing feature, you probably wouldn't say they had brown hair! Similarly, lots of music is fast or loud or lively: try to find the most interesting and distinctive features to describe your chosen music. The most original musical features are easier to remember, too!

Listen to one of your chosen pieces, and identify three musical features.

Name of piece _____

Musical Feature 1 _____

What type of feature is this, from the list below?

Rhythmic	☐	Melodic	☐
Tempo (or tempo changes)	☐	Harmonic	☐
Tonality	☐	Instrumentation	☐
Texture	☐	Mood	☐
Structure/Form	☐	Other: _____	☐

Explain or define the feature:

_____

_____

Describe the musical feature, referring to where it is illustrated in your chosen music and lyrics. This will show that you know the music well.

_____

_____

_____

Musical Feature 2 _____

What type of feature is this? (Consult the list above.) _____

Explain or define the feature:

_____

_____

_____

Describe the musical feature, referring to where it is illustrated in your chosen music and lyrics. This will show that you know the music well.

_____

_____

_____

Musical Feature 3 _____

What type of feature is this? (Consult the list on the previous page.)

_____

Explain or define the feature:

_____

_____

Describe the musical feature, referring to where it is illustrated in your chosen music and lyrics. This will show that you know the music well.

_____

_____

_____

Compare the two pieces of music you chose, explaining how they are similar and how they are different.

_____

_____

_____

_____

What is your personal opinion or response to the music (as a musician, thinking about musical features)? List your points below:

_____

_____

_____

_____

_____

Exam hints

- Sometimes the examination question (Question 10 at Higher Level and Question 8 at Ordinary Level) asks you to present your chosen general study topic as a radio programme, or to describe the music to students in your school. This is your chance to be creative and to keep the interest of your audience. You need to find music that is engaging and different and appealing to listeners.

- To prepare for this, it would be useful to do a presentation for your class where you introduce the music, just like a DJ or programme presenter. Begin with some interesting background information that might get their attention. Then talk about the musical features they might like to listen out for during the presentation.

- If you can record this as a video or DVD it would really help you to become an expert on your topic, and you would remember it all for the exam as well.

Irish Traditional Songs

(see Core Book page 86)

In the syllabus, the full title of this category is: **'Accompanied and unaccompanied traditional Irish songs with Irish or English texts, including arrangements by modern Irish composers'**.

She Moved Through the Fair

(Core Book page 87)

The composer is unknown, but Herbert Hughes collected this song in Donegal. Look at the score and follow it as you listen to the recording. Then answer the questions below.

1 What is the key of the music? _____

2 What are the letter names of the notes in bar 4?

3 One of the three notes is flattened: it is a semitone below the major scale equivalent. Which degree of the scale is it?

_____

4 This is then called a flattened s __ __ __ __ __ __ , a feature of traditional Irish music.

5 There are four phrases. The first is labelled A on the score, and the second is B. Complete the form or structure of the song by filling in the boxes on the score for the third and fourth phrases.

6 This form is: Ternary ☐   Binary ☐ _____

7 Circle an example of ornamentation on the score and write the bar number here _____

8 Highlight the lowest note and the highest note on the score. Write the two notes on the stave below.

9 What is the range of the song? _____

10 List three important features of Irish music found in this song.

(a) _____

(b) _____

(c) _____

Listen again to the Mary Black version of 'She Moved Through the Fair' on the CD.

© Redferns

11 This performance of the verse is:

Accompanied ☐   Unaccompanied ☐

12 It is performed in: Strict rhythm ☐   Free rhythm ☐

13 Mary Black sings this in sean-nós style. Learn more about her by looking up her website. www.mary-black.net

Use a Revision Song Box to record important details. You will find this on page 88; please photocopy this page as many times as you need to.

Mary Black

'Sí Do Mhaimeo Í

(Core Book page 87)

Listen to the track on the CD, look at the printed music and answer the following questions.

Refrain

'Sí do Mhai - meo   í,   'sí do Mhai-meo___   í,   'Sí do Mhai - meo   í,   cail - leach an air - (i) - gid;

'Sí do Mhai-meo í,   ó   Bhail' lor- rais Mhóir___   í   'S chuir-feadh sí cóis - tí   'r bhói - thre Chois Fhar- rai - ge!

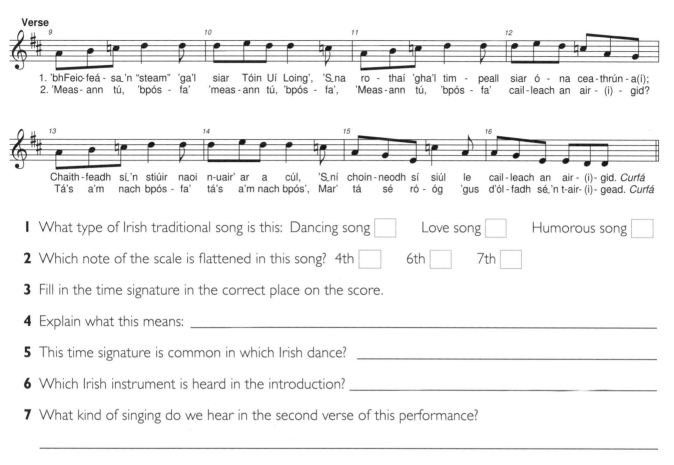

Verse

1. 'bhFeic-feá-sa 'n "steam" 'ga'l siar Tóin Uí Loing', 'S na ro-thaí 'gha'l tim-peall siar ó-na cea-thrún-a(í);
2. 'Meas-ann tú, 'bpós-fa' 'meas-ann tú, 'bpós-fa', 'Meas-ann tú, 'bpós-fa' cail-leach an air-(i)-gid?

Chaith-feadh sí 'n stiúir naoi n-uair' ar a cúl, 'S ní choin-neodh sí siúl le cail-leach an air-(i)-gid. *Curfá*
Tá's a'm nach bpós-fa' tá's a'm nach bpós', Mar' tá sé ró-óg 'gus d'ól-fadh sé 'n t-air-(i)-gead. *Curfá*

1 What type of Irish traditional song is this: Dancing song ☐ Love song ☐ Humorous song ☐

2 Which note of the scale is flattened in this song? 4th ☐ 6th ☐ 7th ☐

3 Fill in the time signature in the correct place on the score.

4 Explain what this means: _____

5 This time signature is common in which Irish dance? _____

6 Which Irish instrument is heard in the introduction? _____

7 What kind of singing do we hear in the second verse of this performance?

_____

8 The performer in this recording, Lasairfhiona Ni Chonaola is a young Irish traditional singer. Find out about her by visiting her website www.aransinger.com

Use a Revision Song Box to record important details – see page 88.

Folksongs from Other Countries (see Core Book page 88)

In the syllabus, the full title of this category is: **'Folksongs from other countries in translation or in the language of origin'.**

All Through the Night

(Core Book page 88)

Follow the score as you listen to the recording. Then answer the questions on the next page.

Sleep a-while and peace attend thee all through the night Guard-ian an-gels

God will lend thee all through the night Soft the dream-y hours are creep-ing

hill and vale in slum-ber sleep-ing God a-lone his watch is keep-ing all through the night

1 The introduction is hummed by: Female choir ☐   Male Choir ☐   Children's choir ☐

2 Verse I is sung by: Male solo ☐   Female solo ☐   Treble voice ☐

3 Suggest a suitable tempo for the music, and write it in the correct place on the score.

4 Follow the score again as you listen to the verse, starting at **00:20**. Fill in the form in the boxes provided over the score, using the letters A and B.

5 What word describes this form: Binary ☐   Ternary ☐

6 The melody moves: Mostly by step ☐   Mostly by leap ☐

7 A boy's choir sings above the solo melody in verse 2 (bars 1–8), starting at **01:22**. It becomes clearly audible from **01:34**. This is called a: D __ __ __ __ __ __ .

8 What happens in bars 9–12 in verse 2 (starting at **01:48**)?

_____

9 What instrument joins the accompaniment in verse 3 (**02:28**)? O __ __ __ __

10 Describe the ending of the song. How does this suit the mood and lyrics of the song?

_____

_____

Use a Revision Song Box to record important details – see page 88.

Lord of the Dance

The words and melody are shown on page 89 of the Core Book.

Listen to the track on the CD and answer the following questions.

1 Name a percussion instrument heard in the introduction: _____

2 What instrumental technique can be heard on the strings in the introduction, starting at **00:08**?

_____

3 Starting at **00:14**, verse I is sung by: Female voices ☐   Male voices ☐   Treble voices ☐

4 What happens in the first chorus (starting **00:27**)?

_____

_____

5 Verse 2 (**00:43**) is sung by: _____

The words for verse 3 are as follows:

I danced on the Sabbath and I cured the lame,
The holy people said it was a shame,
They whipped and they stripped and they hung me high
And they left me there on a cross to die.

6 Describe verse 3 (**01:12**). How does the music reflect the mood of the lyrics?

_____

_____

Use a Revision Song Box to record important details – see page 88.

The Banana Boat Song

The words and melody are shown on pages 90–91 of the Core Book.

Listen to the track on the CD and answer the following questions.

1 The song begins with a slow introduction sung by: Solo female voice ☐ Solo male voice ☐

2 What type of instrument accompanies the introduction? _____

3 The verse begins at **00:28**. What sort of structure does it have?

Ternary ☐   Binary ☐   Call and Response ☐

4 Describe the background to this song.

_____

_____

_____

Use a Revision Song Box to record important details – see page 88.

Art Songs

(see Core Book page 91)

In the syllabus, the full title of this category is: **'Art songs composed by the great masters and recognised twentieth century composers'.**

1 What is the German name for an art song? L __ __ __

2 What structure describes a song that uses the same music for every verse? S __ __ __ __ __ __ __ .

3 What structure describes a song with different music throughout?
   T __ __ __ __ __ __ - C __ __ __ __ __ __ __ .

Art Song Crossword

Across

2. A setting of a poem to music (3, 4)

5. This structure has different music throughout the song. (7, 8)

Down

1. This structure has the same music for every verse. (8)

3. The atmosphere created in the song. (4)

4. A German art song (4)

Die Forelle (The Trout)   *Schubert*

(Core Book page 92)

This is a Lied, a German art song. It tells the story of a trout in a little river, eventually caught by a fisherman. The music and words are on page 92 of the Core Book. Listen to the track on the CD and answer the following questions.

00:00–00:06

1 How does the piano part in the introduction set the scene for the song?

_____

Verse 1   00:07–00:34

2 The mood of verse 1 is: Sad ☐   Happy ☐   Peaceful ☐

Verse 2   00:40–1:08

Verse 3   01:14–1:48

3 The mood changes in verse 3. It becomes: Dramatic ☐   Calm ☐

4 What is the tonality of the beginning of verse 3? Why do you think this is?

_____

_____

5 At **01:23** the rippling motif seems to disappear. Why might this be?

_____

_____

6 At the very end, the dynamics in the piano accompaniment are:

Loud (**f**) ☐   Moderately loud (**mf**) ☐   Very soft (**pp**) ☐

Use a Revision Song Box to record important details – see page 88.

Heidenröslein (Hedge Roses)   *Schubert*

(Core Book page 93)

This is another Lied. The music and words are on page 93 of the Core Book. Listen to the track on the CD and answer the following questions.

1 What language is the recording sung in? Why?

_____

_____

_____

_____

2 Give one melodic feature of the song. _____

_____

3 This song has a key change in the middle. Another name for this is M __ __ __ __ __ __ __ __ __ __ .

4 The singer has dramatic pauses in each verse. How is that shown in the musical score?

_____

5 The tempo in the song: Stays the same throughout ☐   Slows down and speeds up ☐

Use a Revision Song Box to record important details – see page 88.

Wiegenlied (Lullaby)

Brahms

(Core Book page 94)

Listen to the track on the CD and answer the following questions.

1 What is the mood of the song? _____

_____

2 The form is shown by the letters A B C C₁. How is the second C phrase different from the first?

_____

_____

3 What leap does the third phrase begin on?

A leap of a 5th ☐   A leap of an octave ☐   A leap of a 6th ☐

Use a Revision Song Box to record important details – see page 88.

Historical and Modern Ballads

(see Core Book page 94)

Fields of Athenry

Pete St. John

(Core Book page 94)

Listen to the track on the CD and answer the following questions.

1 The introduction to the song is played by:

Guitar and Bassoon ☐   Harp and Viola ☐   Cello and Guitar ☐

2 The melody line in the introduction is from the:

First line of the verse ☐   First line of the chorus ☐   Last line of the verse and chorus ☐

3 Verse 1 is sung by: Male solo voice ☐   Female solo voice ☐

4 Which instrumental section joins in to accompany the chorus? Strings ☐   Brass ☐   Percussion ☐

Use a Revision Song Box to record important details – see page 88.

Isle of Inisfree

Richard Farrelly

(Core Book page 96)

Listen to the track on the CD and answer the following questions.

1 The introduction is played by: Organ ☐   Piano ☐   Celeste ☐

2 The form of the verse is: AA₁AA₁BA₁ ☐   ABABAA ☐   ABCBCA ☐

3 The mood of the music is: _____

4 Which famous film features this melody in the soundtrack?

_____

Use a Revision Song Box to record important details – see page 88.

This Land is Your Land

Woody Guthrie

(Core Book page 98)

Listen to the track on the CD and answer the following questions.

Bright and cheerful

This land is   your land,_____ this land_ is
walk - ing_____ that rib - bon of

my   land,_____ from Cal - i - for - nia_____ to the New York   is - land;____
high - way_____   I saw a - bove   me_____ that_ end - less sky - way;____

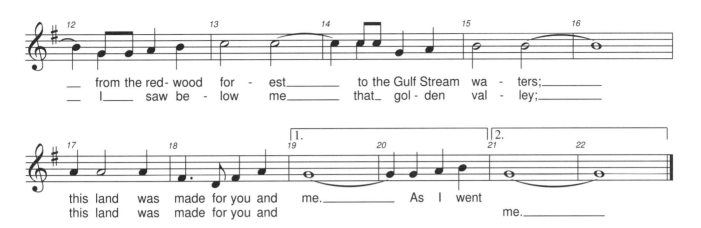

_ from the red- wood for - est_____ to the Gulf Stream wa - ters;_____
_ I_ saw be - low me_____ that_ gol - den val - ley;_____

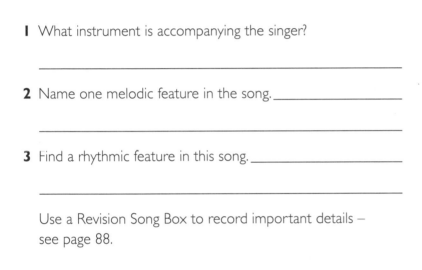

this land was made for you and me._____ As I went
this land was made for you and me._____

1 What instrument is accompanying the singer?

_____

2 Name one melodic feature in the song. _____

_____

3 Find a rhythmic feature in this song. _____

_____

Use a Revision Song Box to record important details –
see page 88.

Woody Guthrie

© Getty Images

Popular Songs

In the syllabus, the full title of this category is: **'Popular songs including negro spirituals, jazz and blues songs'. See the Core Book pages 99 and 104–5.**

Rock Around the Clock
as performed by Bill Haley and his Comets

(Core Book page 103)

Listen to the track on the CD and answer the following questions.

00:00–00:11

1 Listening to the solo voice in the introduction, what melodic feature can you identify?

_____

Verse 1 00:11–00:27

2 The opening phrase features: Upward triadic movement ☐   An upward scale ☐

Verse 2 00:27–00:42

3 Which flattened notes do all the verses contain? Flattened 3rd and 7th ☐   Flattened 3rd and 4th ☐

Instrumental break   00:43–00:58

4 Which instrument plays the instrumental break after verse 2? Give a short description of the break.

_____

_____

5 The instrumental is accompanied by: _____ and _____ .

Verse 3   00:58–01:14

Verse 4   01:14–01:30

Instrumental break   01:30–01:45

6 Another instrumental break occurs after verse 4, at **01:30**. This features:

Trumpet and trombone ☐   Saxophone and guitar ☐

Verse 5   01:45–01:59

Ending   01: 59–02:08

7 The very last sound we hear, at **2:06**, is made by which instrument? _____

8 What is the harmonic basis for the song?   12-bar blues progressions ☐   Classical progressions ☐

Use a Revision Song Box to record important details – see page 88.

When the Saints Go Marching In   *as performed by Louis Armstrong*

(Core Book page 104)

Listen to the track on the CD and answer the following questions.

Spoken introduction   00:04–00:18

00:18–00:36

I Which instrument introduces the tune, from **00:18** to **00:36**?

Saxophone ☐

Trumpet ☐

Trombone ☐

00:41–00:59

2 This verse is sung by Louis Armstrong. What happens at the end of each phrase, at **00:43**, **00:45** and **00:50**?

_____

00:41–00:59

3 Name the instrument playing the break after the sung verse:

_____

Use a Revision Song Box to record important details – see page 88.

I Wish I Knew How It Would Feel To Be Free

(Core Book page 105)

as performed by Nina Simone

Listen to the track on the CD and answer the following questions.

The full words of the song are on page 105 of the Core Book.

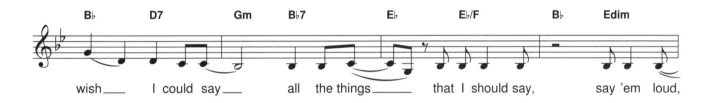

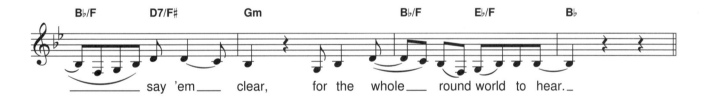

1 The song begins with a long introduction played on the: _____

2 Identify a rhythmic feature in the song. _____

3 What instrument joins in when the vocal part starts, maintaining a strong rhythm? _____

4 Identify a melodic feature in this song. _____

Use a Revision Song Box to record important details – see page 88.

Church Music and Carols

(see Core Book page 106)

In the syllabus, the full title of this category is: **'Accompanied and unaccompanied vocal church music and carols'.**

Alleluia

(Core Book page 106) Please note: this is a different piece from the 'Alleluia' by Mozart – see page 86.

Listen to the track on the CD and answer the following questions.

Al - le - lú - ia,   al - le - lú - ia, ___ al - le - lú - ia.

1 What type of music is this? _____

2 Why are there no barlines? _____

_____

3 This performance is: Accompanied ☐   Unaccompanied ☐

4 What is the texture of this music? Homophonic ☐   Polyphonic ☐   Monophonic ☐

5 The text setting is: Syllabic ☐   Melismatic ☐   A mixture of syllabic and melismatic ☐

Use a Revision Song Box to record important details – see page 88.

The Weaver

Liam Lawton

(Core Book page 106)

Listen to the track on the CD and answer the following questions.

Verse 1   00:06–00:36

1 In verse 1, the vocal part is performed by: Solo voice ☐   Vocal duet ☐   Choral Group ☐

Verse 1   00:36–01:05

2 In verse 2, the vocal part is performed by: Solo voice ☐   Vocal duet ☐   Choral group ☐

3 Which instruments join in, or play louder, in the accompaniment in verse 2?

_____

Verse 3   01:05–01:35

4 Describe the vocal performers here: _____

_____

Instrumental break   01:35–02:25

5 The instrumental is played by: Accordion ☐   Uilleann pipes ☐   Concertina ☐

6 At **02:00** another instrument joins: Flute ☐   Fiddle ☐   Cello ☐

Verse 4   02:30–03:03

7 Which instrument is added to the texture here? It can be heard clearly just before verse 4 begins, at **02:28**.

_____

8 The very end of the song: Slows and fades ☐   Builds and quickens ☐

Use a Revision Song Box to record important details – see page 88.

Away in a Manger

W. J. Kirkpatrick

(Core Book page 109)

Listen to the track on the CD and answer the following questions.

A - way   in   a ___   man - ger,   no ___   crib   for   a   bed,   the ___

lit - tle   Lord   Je - sus   laid ___   down   his   sweet   head.   The

stars   in   the ___   bright   sky   looked ___   down   where   he   lay,   the ___

lit - tle   Lord   Je - sus   a - sleep   on   the   hay.

1 What key is this music in: Key of G major ☐   Key of F major ☐   Key of C minor ☐

2 The introduction is played by: Piano ☐   Harp ☐   Celeste ☐

3 Name one rhythmic feature found at the beginning of the melody. How does it start?

_____

_____

4 The mood of the song is: _____

5 The interlude between verses 1 and 2 is played by: Clarinet ☐   Flute ☐   Recorder ☐

Use a Revision Song Box to record important details – see page 88.

Songs from Operas, Operettas, Oratorios, Cantatas and Stage Musicals

(see Core Book page 110)

La Donna è Mobile from *Rigoletto*

Verdi

(Core Book page 111, with a recorder version on page 10)

Listen to the track on the CD and answer the following questions.

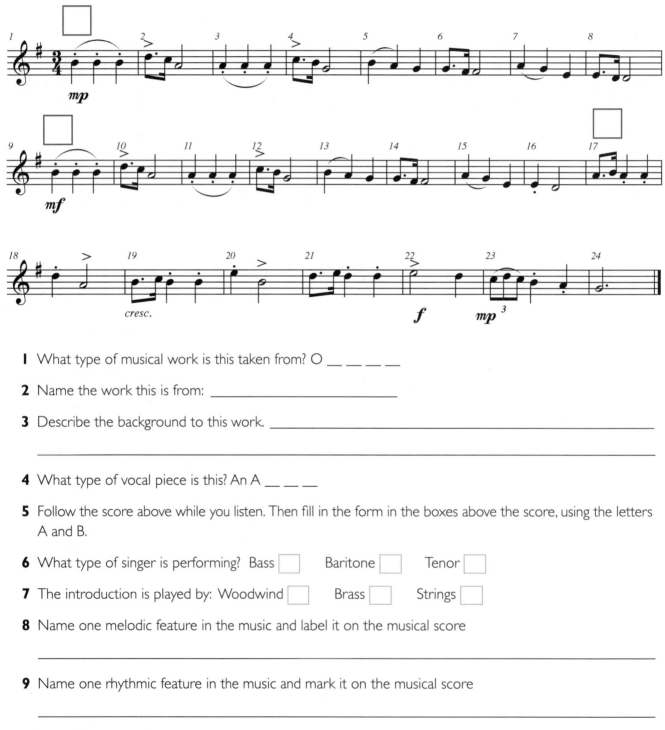

1 What type of musical work is this taken from? O __ __ __ __

2 Name the work this is from: _____

3 Describe the background to this work. _____

_____

4 What type of vocal piece is this? An A __ __ __

5 Follow the score above while you listen. Then fill in the form in the boxes above the score, using the letters A and B.

6 What type of singer is performing? Bass ☐   Baritone ☐   Tenor ☐

7 The introduction is played by: Woodwind ☐   Brass ☐   Strings ☐

8 Name one melodic feature in the music and label it on the musical score

_____

9 Name one rhythmic feature in the music and mark it on the musical score

_____

Use a Revision Song Box to record important details – see page 88.

Jesu, Joy of Man's Desiring from Cantata 147   *Bach*

(Core Book pages 111–114)

Listen to the track on the CD and answer the following questions.

1 What type of musical work is this taken from? _____

2 Name the work this is from: _____

3 Which of these rhythmic features can you identify in the introduction:

Dotted rhythm ☐   Triplets ☐   Syncopation ☐

4 The main theme (starting at **00:21**) is based on a: Folk tune ☐   German chorale tune ☐

5 The main theme is sung by: Solo tenor ☐   Solo soprano ☐   Choir ☐

6 How does the new melody contrast with the instrumental accompaniment?

_____

_____

Use a Revision Song Box to record important details – see page 88.

We Go Together from

Grease *Warren Casey and Jim Jacobs*

(Core Book page 114)

Listen to the track on the CD and answer the following questions.

1 What type of musical work is this taken from?

_____

2 Name the work this is from:

_____

3 What is the mood of the music?

_____

_____

4 Complete this diagram of the structure of this song:

00:00	00:08	00:26	00:43	01:00	01:29	01:46	02.03
Intro	**Verse I**	_____	**Bridge**	_____	_____	_____	**Coda/Outro**
8 bars	16 bars	___ bars	16 bars	26 bars	___ bars	16 bars	48 bars +

5 What instrument plays the solo instrumental? _____

Use a Revision Song Box to record important details – see page 88.

Rounds and Canons, Descants, Part Songs

(see Core Book page 116)

In the syllabus, the full title of this category is: **'Songs involving simple descants, ostinati, simple two part songs, rounds and canons'.**

Alleluia

Mozart

(Core Book page 116) Please note: this is a different piece from the plainsong 'Alleluia' – see page 82. Look at the music and lyrics, sing the piece with your class and answer the following questions.

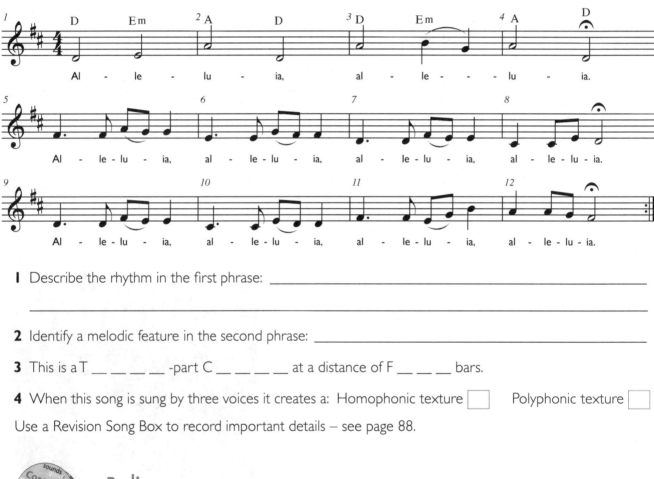

1 Describe the rhythm in the first phrase: _____

_____

2 Identify a melodic feature in the second phrase: _____

3 This is a T __ __ __ __ -part C __ __ __ __ at a distance of F __ __ __ bars.

4 When this song is sung by three voices it creates a: Homophonic texture ☐   Polyphonic texture ☐

Use a Revision Song Box to record important details – see page 88.

Believe

Lin Marsh

(Core Book page 117) The words and music are shown on pages 117–119 of the Core Book.

Listen to the track on the CD and answer the following questions.

1 This song begins with the singers in unison. Identify one rhythmic feature of this verse:

_____

2 Identify one melodic feature: _____

3 In verse 2, starting at **01:13**, harmony is added by backing vocals humming above the melodic line. This is called a D __ __ __ __ __ __ .

4 What percussion can you identify in this piece? _____

Use a Revision Song Box to record important details – see page 88.

Calypso

Jan Holdstock

(Core Book page 119)

Look at this music and lyrics, sing this piece with your class and answer the questions.

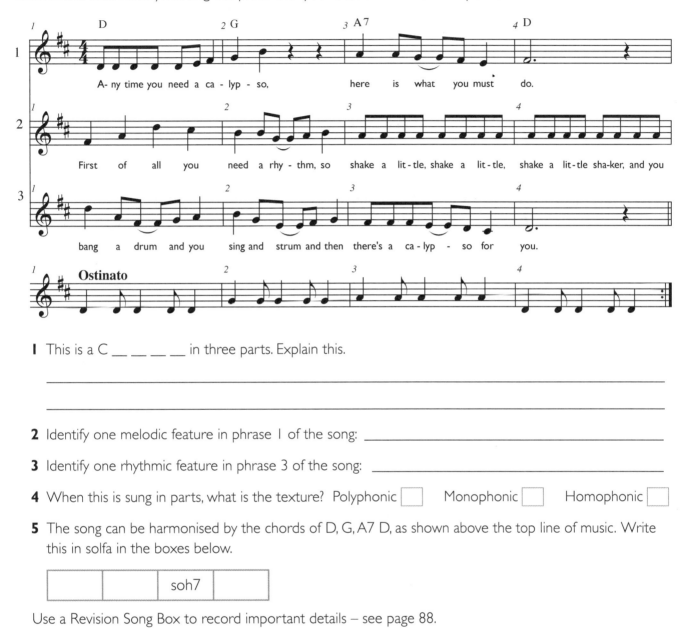

1 This is a C __ __ __ __ in three parts. Explain this.

_____

_____

2 Identify one melodic feature in phrase 1 of the song: _____

3 Identify one rhythmic feature in phrase 3 of the song: _____

4 When this is sung in parts, what is the texture? Polyphonic ☐   Monophonic ☐   Homophonic ☐

5 The song can be harmonised by the chords of D, G, A7 D, as shown above the top line of music. Write this in solfa in the boxes below.

		soh7	

Use a Revision Song Box to record important details – see page 88.

Dona Nobis Pacem

Mary Lynn Lightfoot

(Core Book page 119)

Listen to the track on the CD and answer the following questions.

The words and music are shown on pages 119–120 of the Core Book.

1 What is the mood of this song? _____

2 What solo instrument plays the melody in the introduction? _____

3 The choir performing is a: Male voice choir ☐   Mixed choir ☐   Children's choir ☐

Revision Song Boxes — Choice Songs

Please photocopy this page and use the boxes to prepare for Choice Song question.

Use this Revision Song Box to record some important details, especially if this is your Choice Song.

Category of Song: _____

Title of the song: _____

Composer and/or **performer** and/or **country of origin**: _____

_____

_____

Main musical features (These should be memorable, and as unique to the song as possible. You should show you really know the song well.):

_____

_____

_____

_____

_____

_____

_____

_____

Use this Revision Song Box to record some important details, especially if this is your Choice Song.

Category of Song: _____

Title of the song: _____

Composer and/or **performer** and/or **country of origin**: _____

_____

_____

Main musical features (These should be memorable, and as unique to the song as possible. You should show you really know the song well.):

_____

_____

_____

_____

_____

_____

8 | Irish Music

Characteristics of Irish Music

Táimse im' Chodladh

Listen to this song as sung by Zoë Conway, and follow the score.

> In this type of song, the score is a skeleton of the original tune. In the sean-nós style of singing, the vocalist decorates or ornaments the melody.

Tráth - nói - nín___ déa - nach i gcéin cois - lea- sa dom,

Táim - se im' chod - ladh 's ná___ dúis - tear mé; Sea___

dhearc - as lem'___ thaobh an___ spéir - bhean mhais- ea - mháil,

Táim - se im' chod - ladh___ 's ná___ dúis - tear mé. Ba___

bha - chall - ach péar - lach___ dréim - reach barr - (a)- chas A

ca - r(a)n - fholt craobh - ach ag teacht léi ar baill - i- crith, 'S í ag

caith - eamh na saighead trím___ thaobh a___ chea- lag mé,

Táim - se im' chod - ladh___ 's ná___ dúis - tear mé.

I Listen again, carefully following the score, and circle the places in the score where Zoë ornaments the tune.

2 How many places did you mark? _____

3 The music begins on: An upbeat ☐   A downbeat ☐

4 The end of the first phrase (bars 7–8) has a typical Irish music feature. Can you name it?

_____

5 Give the bar numbers where this feature appears again. _____ and _____

6 This verse has some accompaniment which is a non-traditional feature. Describe the accompaniment.

_____

_____

7 This is an **aisling.** Explain what this means in Irish song repertoire.

_____

_____

Sean-nós Singing

Write about some of the features of **sean-nós** singing. You can read about this style on page 138 of the Core Book.

_____

_____

_____

_____

_____

Máiréad Ní Mhaonaigh

© Redferns

Types of Irish Songs

Patriotic Aisling
Drinking Macaronic Carols
Humorous Working
Lullabies Dandling
Lament Love Religious

Look at this visual of all the types of Irish songs. In the boxes on the opposite page, write a few bullet points about each, and find a good example, as shown in the first box.

Type of song: Lament
A slow plaintive song
- Tells of loss
- Death, eviction, emigration
- Called a caoine in Irish

Example: 'Anach Cuain'. This tells of a tragedy in Mayo when a boat sinks and the people and sheep on board drown.

Type of song: Lament
A slow plaintive song
- Tells of loss
- Death, eviction, emigration

Irish Dances

1 Complete the following chart to illustrate the most typical form or structure of Irish dances (See Core Book page 124).

A			
8 Bars			8 Bars
		Turn	

2 Complete the chart below, showing types of dances and their characteristics. Look at pages 124–129 of the Core Book to help you complete this.

Type of Dance	Time Signature	Typical Bar of Rhythm	Example
Jig		♩ ♪ ♫♩	
Slip jig			
Reel			
Hornpipe			

3 Name that dance!

Listen to the following short excerpts of Irish Dances and identify the dance. (When you have corrected these with your teacher you can use them as a resource to get familiar with the dances)

(a) Jig ☐   Reel ☐
Hornpipe ☐   Slip Jig ☐

Name: _____

(b) Jig ☐   Reel ☐
Hornpipe ☐   Slip Jig ☐

Name: _____

(c) Track 10

Jig ☐   Reel ☐
Hornpipe ☐   Slip Jig ☐

Name: _____

(d) Track 11

Jig ☐   Reel ☐
Hornpipe ☐   Slip Jig ☐

Name: _____

(e) Track 12

Jig ☐   Reel ☐
Hornpipe ☐   Slip Jig ☐

Name: _____

(f) Track 13

Jig ☐   Reel ☐
Hornpipe ☐   Slip Jig ☐

Name: _____

(g) Track 14

Jig ☐   Reel ☐
Hornpipe ☐   Slip Jig ☐

Name: _____

(h) Track 15

Jig ☐   Reel ☐
Hornpipe ☐   Slip Jig ☐

Name: _____

(i) Track 16

Jig ☐   Reel ☐
Hornpipe ☐   Slip Jig ☐

Name: _____

(j) Track 17

Jig ☐   Reel ☐
Hornpipe ☐   Slip Jig ☐

Name: _____

(k) Track 18

Jig ☐   Reel ☐
Hornpipe ☐   Slip Jig ☐

Name: _____

(l) Track 19

Jig ☐   Reel ☐
Hornpipe ☐   Slip Jig ☐

Name: _____

Track 20

The Hole in the Hedge/Seamus Cooley's Jig

Listen to this music played by Martin Hayes, and answer the following questions.

1 Which dance is Martin playing? Jig ☐   Reel ☐   Hornpipe ☐   Slip Jig ☐

2 What kind of musical influences can you hear in this piece? Jazz ☐   Classical ☐   Popular ☐

3 This music has: No ornamentation ☐   Ornamentation ☐

4 How many tunes are in the set played here? _____

5 How would you describe the music?

_____

6 Research Martin Hayes on his website www.martinhayes.com and write a note on his musical influences.

_____

_____

_____

Instruments and Performers in Irish Music

See Core Book pages 125–132.

1 Look at the instruments shown below. Name each instrument, and write a short note on each. Imagine you are explaining them to an alien from Mars – state the obvious points clearly!

2 For each instrument, give two examples of well-known performers.

E

© Lebrecht Music and Arts Photo Library/Alamy

F

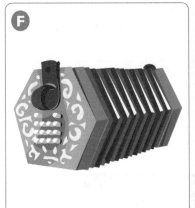

© Roberta Cotter

G

© Stephen Power/Alamy

3 Identify these percussion instruments used in Irish music:

The Harping Tradition

See Core Book pages 133–4.

I Look at this comic illustration about **Turlough O'Carolan** and the harping tradition, and fill in the story.

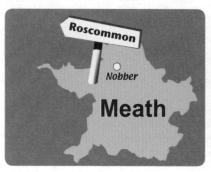

_____

_____

_____

_____

_____

_____

_____

_____

_____

_____

_____

_____

2 Look at the comic illustration of the **Belfast Harp Festival** below and fill in the story.

_____   _____   _____
_____   _____   _____
_____   _____   _____
_____   _____   _____
_____   _____   _____

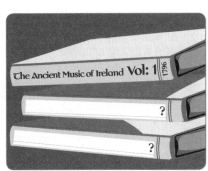

_____   _____   _____
_____   _____   _____
_____   _____   _____
_____   _____   _____
_____   _____   _____

Listening Questions

Blackbird

Listen to this performance by Sharon Shannon and answer the questions.

1 What instrument begins with chordal accompaniment?_____

2 What solo instrument plays the melody? _____

3 Something happens at **01:25**. Describe the change in the music at this point.

_____
_____

Carolan's Concerto

Listen to this performance by Janet Harbison of *Carolan's Concerto* and answer the questions.

1 What instrument is playing here? _____

2 What kind of music influenced this composition? Jazz ☐   Classical ☐   Popular ☐

3 Describe the tempo of the music: _____

St Patrick's Day

Listen to this performance by the Gallowglas Céilí Band. and answer the questions.

See the tune on page 140.

1 Write a short note about the tradition of céilí music. You can read about céilí music and dancing on page 132 of the Core Book.

_____

_____

_____

_____

_____

_____

_____

2 What instrument is playing the melody at the beginning? Fiddle ☐   Accordion ☐   Flute ☐

3 What percussion instrument associated with céilí music is playing here? _____

4 What metre does the music have? 2 ☐   3 ☐   4 ☐

Lots of Drops of Brandy

Listen to this performance by the Chieftains and answer the questions.

00:00

1 What instrument begins the piece? _____

00:05

2 What instrument joins in playing a drone? Piano ☐   Uilleann pipes ☐   Cello ☐

00:09

3 The first time we hear the tune it is played in jig time. List the instruments as they enter in the phrase plan below:

A 00:09 _____

A 00:17 _____

B 00:25 _____

B 00:33 _____

01:11

4 The second jig opens with a different instrument. What is it? _____

02:09

5 What is the dance rhythm here? _____

6 Write a typical bar of rhythm for this dance: _____

02:42

7 The final dance returns to the rhythm of the original traditional tune. What type of dance is this?

_____

Write a note on the Chieftains and their contribution to Irish Music. Include a brief synopsis of this tune or another you know well.

© Getty Images

_____

_____

_____

_____

Irish Instruments Crossword

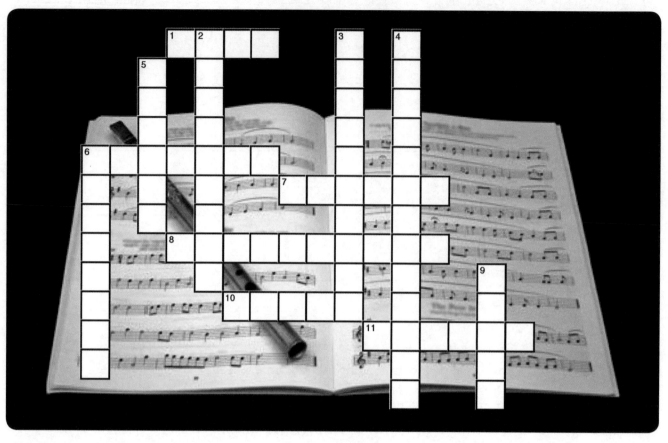

Across

1. This instrument is plucked (4)
6. A circular instrument with a 'head' made of skin (7)
7. Strummed or plucked to add harmonies, used in many traditions (6)
8. A hexagonal instrument with buttons (10)
10. Wooden instrument held sideways (5)
11. Can eat with these for soup or dessert (6)

Down

2. Also nicknamed 'the box' (9)
3. Has six holes and a fipple (3, 7)
4. Free reed instrument with bellows and drone (8, 5)
5. Has four strings and is played with the bow (also has another name, also with six letters) (6)
6. A Greek instrument, adapted for use in Irish music (8)
9. This instrument is plucked and has a round body (5)

Organisations and Educators

1 Write about two organisations that help to promote Irish music nowadays.

(a) _____

_____

_____

(b) _____

_____

_____

2 Write a note on Seán Ó Riada and his contribution to Irish music.

_____

_____

_____

_____

Ag Críost an Síol

Listen to this performance of _Ag Críost an Síol_, by Cór Chúil Aodha and answer the questions.

1 The singers are: Men and boys ☐   Women and men ☐

2 The language is: _____

3 The music is accompanied by: _____

4 The composer is: _____.

You can read more about this composer on pages 138–139 of the Core Book.

Modern Influences

Eleanor Rigby

Listen to this performance by De Danann and answer the questions.

1 The introduction is played by: Flute ☐   Fiddle ☐   Accordion ☐

00:33

2 What instrument plays the melody line here? _____

3 The accompanying harmony instrument is: _____

01:03

4 Name the instrument that joins the melody line here: _____

5 What other instruments can you identify? _____

6 The original tune was composed and performed by which famous group?

_____

Theme from _Harry's Game_

Listen to this track performed by Clannad and answer the questions.

1 What kind of voice begins the piece? Describe the style of singing. _____

_____

2 What musical features here are not typical of Irish music?

_____

_____

3 Find out more about this group, and write some notes on your findings. You can read about them on page 145 of the Core Book.

_____

_____

_____

Idir Eatarthu

Listen to this track performed by Mícheál Ó Súilleabháin and answer the questions.

1 Describe the introduction to this piece:

_____

_____

_____

2 What solo instrument plays the Irish tune? _____

3 What percussion instrument accompanies here? _____

Your Favourites

1 Choose a group that plays Irish music, and do some research into their music, instruments, influences and examples of their pieces. If possible design a comic to illustrate your story.

_____

_____

_____

_____

_____

2 Who is your favourite solo Irish musician? Write about them and their music. If possible design a comic to illustrate your story.

_____

_____

_____

_____

_____

9 | Composing Skills: The Basics

Notes, Beats and Bars

Puzzle Time!

Complete the following exercise and then find your answers in the wordsearch below. Look at Core Book pages 149–154 if you need help.

1 What is the steady beat that underlies a piece of music called? _____

2 What does this symbol mean? > _____

3 Different durations or lengths of sound create a
 _ _ _ _ _ _

4 What type of note is known as a quarter note? _____

5 What type of note is worth half a crotchet?
 _____

6 What type of note is worth two crotchets?
 _____

7 A person who composes music is called a
 _ _ _ _ _ _ _ _

8 A minim is also known as a _ _ _ _ note.

9 What type of note is worth four crotchets?
 _____

10 Music is divided into short sections called
 _ _ _ _

11 A semibreve is also known as a _ _ _ _ _ _ note.

12 What is another name for a bar? _____

13 Bars are divided by bar_ _ _ _ _

14 What type of barline is used to end a piece of music? _____

15 What is another name for $\frac{4}{4}$ time?
 _____

16 What is the symbol called which tells you how many beats should be in each bar?
 _____

17 The _ _ _ number of the time signature tells us how many beats are in each bar.

18 The _ _ _ _ _ _ number of the time signature tells us what type of beat features in each bar.

C	R	O	T	C	H	E	T	I	M	N	R	O
O	O	Q	O	I	D	T	D	B	Q	A	V	Q
M	C	M	P	N	M	Y	O	A	B	C	T	W
P	H	R	M	E	A	S	U	R	E	C	U	S
O	T	H	F	O	T	M	B	L	W	E	B	E
S	T	A	L	R	N	A	L	I	M	N	O	M
E	S	L	U	P	Q	U	E	N	I	T	T	I
R	T	F	F	W	H	O	L	E	N	S	T	B
Q	U	A	V	E	R	R	A	S	I	P	O	R
I	A	T	M	R	H	Y	T	H	M	Q	M	E
H	E	Q	B	A	R	S	N	O	C	A	H	V
T	I	M	E	S	I	G	N	A	T	U	R	E

103

Practice Time!

Practise drawing the different types of notes you need to compose a rhythm. Look at Core Book pages 150–152 if you need help.

Draw a line of **crotchets** – Stems UP on the RIGHT

Draw a line of **crotchets** – Stems DOWN on the LEFT

Draw a line of **quavers** – Stems UP on the RIGHT, tails facing RIGHT

Draw a line of **quavers** – Stems DOWN on the LEFT, tails facing RIGHT

Beam the following notes together to make **pairs of quavers**

Draw a line of **paired quavers** – Stems UP on the RIGHT

Draw a line of **paired quavers** –Stems DOWN on the LEFT

Draw a line of **minims** – Stems UP on the RIGHT

Draw a line of **minims** – Stems DOWN on the LEFT

Add **dots** to the **minims** to create **dotted minims**

Draw a line of **semibreves**

Musical Maths Time

Add up the values of the following notes and select the correct answer

> A crotchet is not *always* the same as a beat, but in this chapter we treat them as the same. So, in the exercises below, **all beats are crotchet beats**.

1 o + o + 𝅗𝅥 =   4 beats ☐   6 beats ☐   10 beats ☐

2 𝅗𝅥 + ♩ + ♩ + ♩ + ♫ =   5 beats ☐   6 beats ☐   7 beats ☐

3 ♩ ♩ + ♩ ♩ + ♩ ♩ + ♩. =   6 beats ☐   8 beats ☐   12 beats ☐

4 ♪ + ♪ + ♪ + ♪ =   1 beats ☐   2 beats ☐   3 beats ☐

5 o + ♩. + ♩ + ♩ + ♪ + ♪ =   10 beats ☐   11 beats ☐   12 beats ☐

Musical Equations

Fill in the missing note to make the following 'musical equations' correct.

1   o + o + ___ = 12 beats

2   ♩ + ___ + ♩ = 5 beats

3   ♩. + ♩. + ___ = 8 beats

4   ♩ ♩ + ___ + ♩ ♩ = 6 beats

5   ♩ + ♩ + ___ + ♩ + ♩ + ♩ + ♩ = 7 beats

True or False

1   ♩ + ♩. + ♩ = ♩ + ♩ + ♩ + ♩ + ♩ + ♩   True ☐   False ☐

2   o + o + o = ♩ + ♩ + ♩ + ♩   True ☐   False ☐

3   ♩ ♩ + ♩ ♩ + ♩ ♩ = ♩.   True ☐   False ☐

4   ♩ + ♩ + ♩ ♩ = o   True ☐   False ☐

5   o. + o. = ♩ + ♩ + ♩ + o   True ☐   False ☐

Match Up

We've done one for you, to show you how.

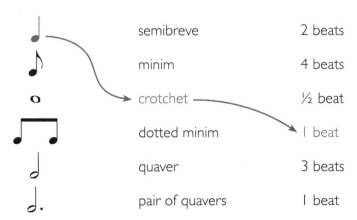

semibreve	2 beats
minim	4 beats
crotchet	½ beat
dotted minim	1 beat
quaver	3 beats
pair of quavers	1 beat

Bars and Time Signatures

In this chapter, we will just use three time signatures:

$$\frac{2}{4} \quad \frac{3}{4} \quad \frac{4}{4}$$

Bars and Barlines

To check that you understand these, read pages 152–154 of the Core Book.

Add barlines to complete the following rhythms. Don't forget to put a double barline at the end. Clue: Check the time signature! The first one has been done for you.

Now draw an **accent** under the strongest beat in each bar, and clap the rhythm.

Time Signatures

Count the beats in each bar and add the correct time signature to each rhythm, at the beginning of the line. Choose from $\frac{2}{4}$, $\frac{3}{4}$ or $\frac{4}{4}$; we won't be using any other time signatures here.

The $\frac{4}{4}$ time signature is also called 'common time', and can be written like this: **C**

Spot the Mistakes

There are lots of things wrong with the examples below – mistakes with the rhythm, or the time signature, or the way the notes are written. Find as many mistakes as you can. Circle all the mistakes you find in red.

Then re-write the rhythms correctly in the space provided below.

Correct version of (1):

Correct version of (2):

Correct version of (3):

Solfa

Solfa is introduced on page 156 of the Core Book.

Sing and Compose: Soh and Mi

Sing the following 4-bar melodies. Try using the handsigns to show the pitches. Only two pitches are used: **soh** and **mi**.

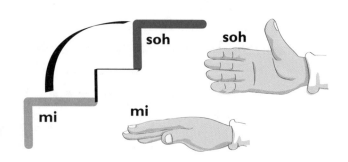

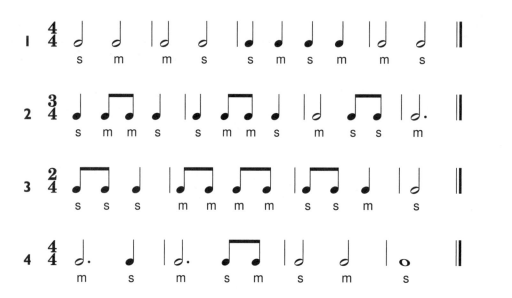

Add your own solfa to the following rhythms and sing them, using the same two notes, soh and mi.

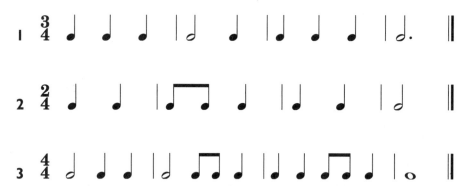

Now compose your own 4-bar rhythms. Add solfa and sing your compositions. Remember to check the time signature at the beginning of your melody.

Rests

These are introduced on page 157 of the Core Book.

> Here is a summary of the rests we have looked at in the Core Book.
> ▬ = semibreve rest; also used as whole bar rest
> ▬ = minim rest   𝄽 = crotchet rest   𝄾 = quaver rest

Identify the following rests and state the value of each rest.

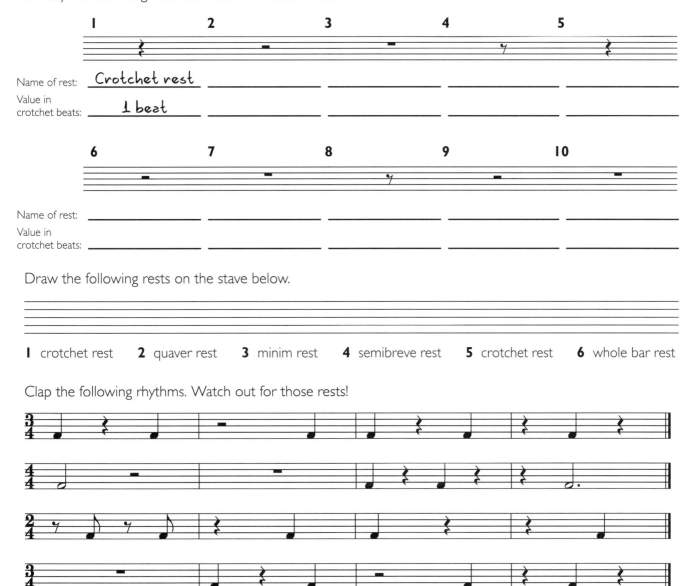

Name of rest: <u>Crotchet rest</u>

Value in crotchet beats: <u>1 beat</u>

Draw the following rests on the stave below.

1 crotchet rest   2 quaver rest   3 minim rest   4 semibreve rest   5 crotchet rest   6 whole bar rest

Clap the following rhythms. Watch out for those rests!

Match Up

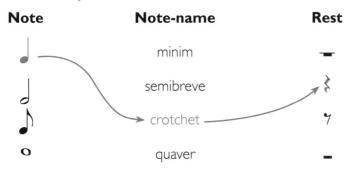

Note	Note-name	Rest

The Treble Clef

1 Fill in the gaps in the Musical Alphabet below. (See Core Book page 158.)

A	B	C	D	E	F	G	A	B	C	D	E	F	G	A	B	C	d	E	F	g

2 Practise drawing treble clefs on the staves below. Core Book page 158 has some advice on how to do this.

3 Can you make up your own rhyme for the lines and spaces when the treble clef is used?

The five lines: **E** **G** **B** **D** **F**

Rhyme:

The four spaces: **F** **A** **C** **E**

Rhyme:

4 Name the notes on the stave below.

Then add stems to the notes to make minims. Remember to follow the rules for drawing stems – see Core Book pages 158–159.

Letter name: B F F C D E g E

Letter name: D C A E g F B F

5 Name the notes. Then beam them together to make pairs of quavers.

Letter name: F E g A F E g A c d F A

Letter name: E C A D f C E A C C

Ledger Lines and Spaces

The notes are not limited to the five lines and four spaces of the treble clef. They can continue above or below, using ledger lines. See Core Book page 159.

Name the following notes.

Letter name: g c c g A d c B c A

Octaves

You have learnt about the **musical alphabet**, how it goes from A to G and then repeats.

The distance from one A to the next one, or one B to the next one, up or down, is called an **octave**. See Core Book page 160.

In the next exercise, draw a note an OCTAVE lower or an OCTAVE higher than the printed note. Then write its letter-name underneath. The first one has been completed for you.

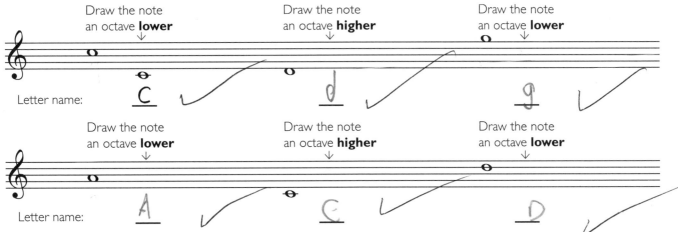

Wordsearch

Here are the clues; they are musical clues! Work out the words on the staves, and then find them in the wordsearch below.

The C on the first ledger line below the treble clef is called **Middle C**.

Writing Notes

Draw the notes on the staves below. First, look at the letter-name you are asked to draw, and check if the note is on a line or space. Then work out where you should put it – on which line or space. Next, look at the type of note you are asked to draw. Then you are ready to draw it.

Here is a reminder of the types of notes.

Semibreve o   **Dotted Minim** o·   **Minim** o   **Crotchet** ♩   **Quaver** ♪

Letter name: C (in a space)   G (on a line)   E (on a line)   B (on a line)
Type of note: crotchet   minim   dotted minim   quaver

Letter name: F (in a space)   Middle C   G (in a space above the stave)   A (on a ledger line)
Type of note: crotchet   semibreve   crotchet   quaver

Letter name: F (on a line)   E (in a space)   D (in a space below the stave)   Middle C
Type of note: dotted minim   semibreve   crotchet   dotted minim

Sing and Compose: Doh, Re, Mi, Soh

Sing these melodies. You could use handsigns here.

1 3/4   d   r   m   s   s   m   r   d

2 4/4   d   r   m   s   s   s   m   r   r   d   d

3 2/4   d   m   s   m   s   s   m   r   r   d

Add your own choice of solfa (Soh, Mi, Re and Doh) to the following rhythms, and sing them. End each tune on Doh.

Now compose your own 4-bar rhythms. Add solfa (Soh, Mi, Re and Doh) and sing your compositions. End each one on Doh, and make it a nice long note to make a clear, cheerful ending.

1 $\frac{3}{4}$ | | | ‖

2 $\frac{4}{4}$ | | | ‖

3 $\frac{2}{4}$ | | | ‖

4 $\frac{3}{4}$ | | | ‖

5 $\frac{4}{4}$ | | | ‖

6 $\frac{2}{4}$ | | | ‖

The Bass Clef

1 Draw a line of bass clefs on the stave below. For help with this, see the advice on page 162 of the Core Book.

2 Circle the incorrect bass clefs on the stave below.

3 Can you make up your own rhyme for the lines and spaces when the bass clef is used?

The five lines:	G	B	D	F	A

Rhyme:

The four spaces:	A	C	E	G

Rhyme:

4 Name the notes on the stave below. Remember it's the bass clef.

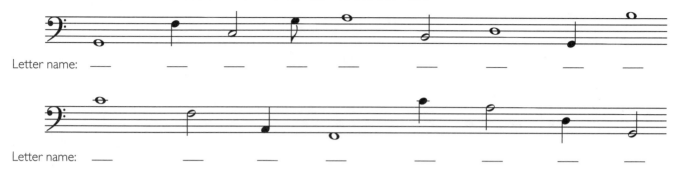

Letter name: ⎯   ⎯   ⎯   ⎯   ⎯   ⎯   ⎯   ⎯   ⎯

Letter name: ⎯   ⎯   ⎯   ⎯   ⎯   ⎯   ⎯   ⎯

5 Draw the notes on the bass clef staves below. Read the instruction, then decide on which line or space the note should go. Then make sure you draw the correct note type.

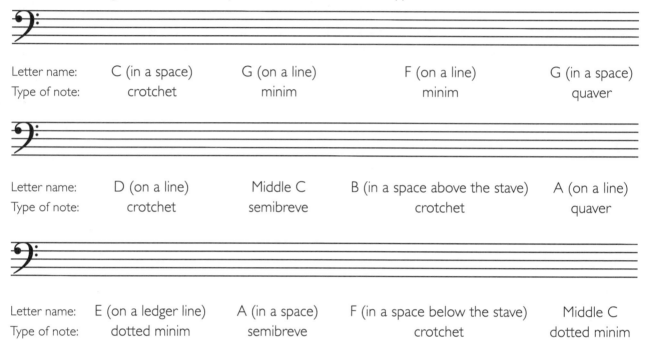

| Letter name: | C (in a space) | G (on a line) | F (on a line) | G (in a space) |
| Type of note: | crotchet | minim | minim | quaver |

| Letter name: | D (on a line) | Middle C | B (in a space above the stave) | A (on a line) |
| Type of note: | crotchet | semibreve | crotchet | quaver |

| Letter name: | E (on a ledger line) | A (in a space) | F (in a space below the stave) | Middle C |
| Type of note: | dotted minim | semibreve | crotchet | dotted minim |

6 Work out the words on these bass clef staves and write them underneath.

7 Name the notes. But this time be careful to check the clef: we have mixed them up!

Story time!

Work out the missing words to complete the story. Check the clefs!

One day my friend ___ and I took a ___ to the zoo. We had to ___ to ___ the lions. We went into the ___ and started to ___ with the smell of rotten ___

The oldest lion was a little

and had no teeth. Instead of

he could only eat ___s and ___!

We ___ him the ___ but

Then had to go because ___ has a ___

___ allergy!

More Sing and Compose

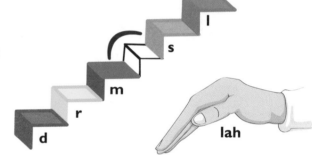

Now we add Lah to Soh, Mi, Re and Doh

Sing the following 4-bar melodies. You could use the handsigns to show the pitches as you sing.

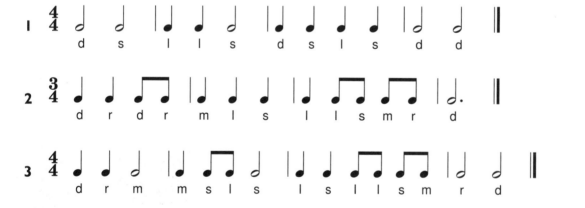

1 d s l l s d s l s d d

2 d r d r m l s l l s m r d

3 d r m m s l s l s l l s m r d

Add your own choice of solfa to the following rhythms and sing the melodies you have composed.

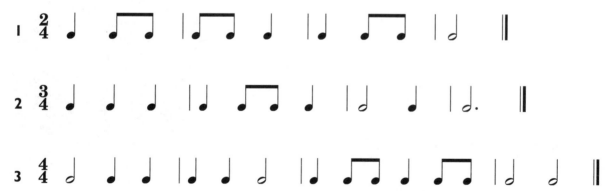

Singing Melodies from the Stave

The following three melodies are written on the stave. Work out the solfa for each, and sing it. The small black box in front of the time signature shows which note is Doh.

Write the following melodies onto the stave. Again, the small black box indicates which note should be Doh.

Now compose your own 4-bar rhythms. Add solfa (d, r, m, s, l) and sing your compositions. It's a good idea to end on a long note.

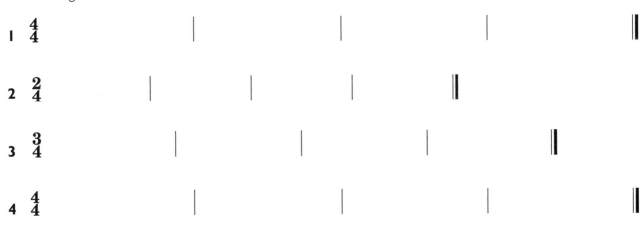

Tones and Semitones See Core Book page 165.

Fill in the blanks in the sentences below.

Here are the words you can choose from. Some of them are used more than once.

Sharp   Natural   Accidentals   Whole   After   Half   Semitone   Flat   Raises   Before   Lowers   Cancels

When you have chosen your missing word for each statement, find your answer in the wordsearch below.

1 The distance from any key on the keyboard to its nearest neighbour is known as a __ __ __ __ __ __ __ __ __.

2 This sign ♯ is a __ __ __ __ __ sign.

3 A semitone may also be called a __ __ __ __ step.

4 Two semitone steps make up a __ __ __ __ __ tone step.

5 A **sharp** sign written before a note __ __ __ __ __ __ the note a __ __ __ __ __ __ __ __ __.

6 When we draw a sharp on the stave it must come __ __ __ __ __ __ the note.

7 When we talk or write about a sharp, it comes __ __ __ __ __ the note.

8 This sign ♭ is a __ __ __ __ sign.

9 A **flat** sign __ __ __ __ __ __ the note a __ __ __ __ __ __ __ __.

10 This sign ♮ is a __ __ __ __ __ __ __ sign. When it is written in front of a note it __ __ __ __ __ __ __ a sharp or flat.

11 Sharps, flats and naturals can also be called __ __ __ __ __ __ __ __ __ __ __.

Sharps and Flats

Sharps are introduced on page 165 of the Core Book, flats on page 166.

1 Name the following notes. Remember to write the sharp AFTER the note name.

2 Raise each note a semitone, by drawing a sharp in front of the note. Then write the name of the note underneath the stave.

3 Draw the following 'sharp' notes. You can choose your own note value. Take care to look at the clef.

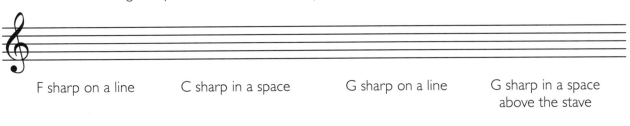

| F sharp on a line | C sharp in a space | G sharp on a line | G sharp in a space above the stave |

| F sharp on a line | G sharp in a space | C sharp in a space | D sharp on a line |

4 Name the following notes.

5 Draw a flat in front of the following notes to LOWER them a semitone.

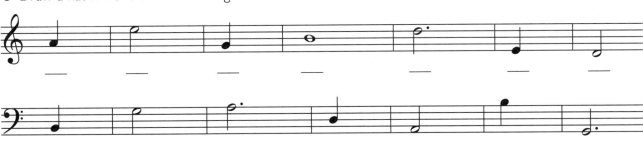

6 Draw the following notes. You can choose your own note value.

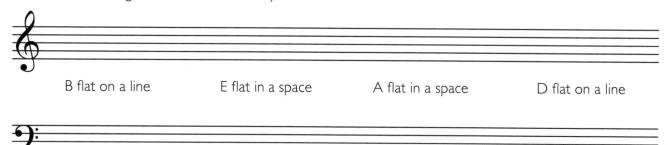

| B flat on a line | E flat in a space | A flat in a space | D flat on a line |

| D flat on a line | E flat in a space | B flat on a line | B flat in a space above the stave |

How can a Note have two Different Names?

To understand sharps and flats, tones and semitones, and how they fit into the major scale, it is helpful to look at a piano keyboard.

Look at the keyboard plan at the top of Core Book page 167. **This will help you to see how all the black notes, and even some of the white notes, can be called by two different note-names.**

When you have understood how it all fits together, test yourself by answering the following questions.

1 Give the SHARP names of the following flat notes. The first one has been done for you.

G flat = F sharp   E flat = [ ]   B flat = [ ]   D flat = [ ]   A flat = [ ]

2 Give the FLAT names of the following sharp notes.

C sharp = D flat   F sharp = [ ]   D sharp = [ ]   A sharp = [ ]   G sharp = [ ]

3 True or False? Are these notes the same or not? Tick the correct box.

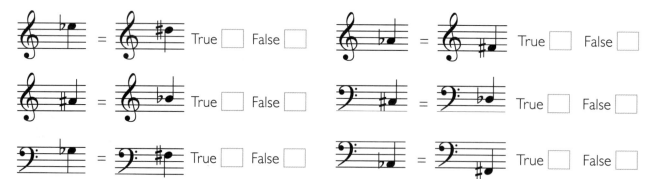

Naturals See Core Book page 167.

1 Name the first note in each bar, then write the same note on the stave but mark it as a natural. Then name that one too. The first bar has been done for you.

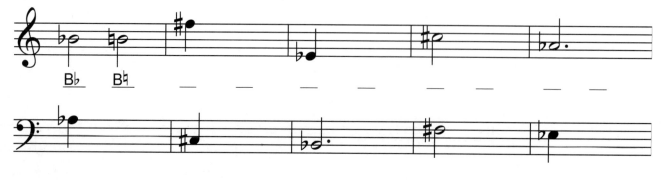

Bb   B♮

2 Draw the following notes.

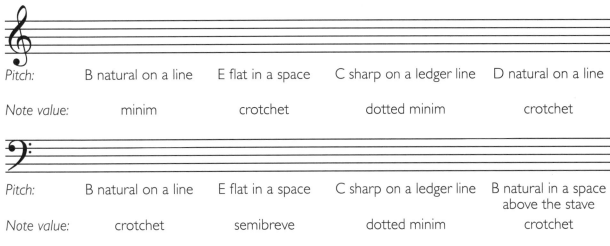

Pitch:	B natural on a line	E flat in a space	C sharp on a ledger line	D natural on a line
Note value:	minim	crotchet	dotted minim	crotchet

Pitch:	B natural on a line	E flat in a space	C sharp on a ledger line	B natural in a space above the stave
Note value:	crotchet	semibreve	dotted minim	crotchet

3 True or False? Are these notes the same or not? Tick the correct box.

More Tones and Semitones See Core Book page 167.

The **Sharp** and **Flat** names of the Treble Clef

The **Sharp** and **Flat** names of the Bass Clef

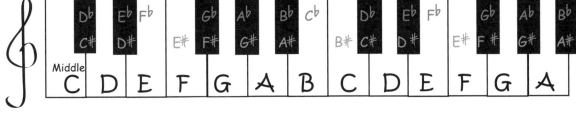

1 Look carefully at the following pairs of notes. Name each note and say whether the distance between each pair is a tone or a semitone. The keyboard plan will help. The first one has been done for you.

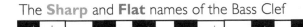
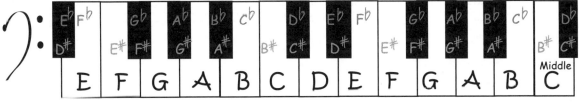

2 True or False? Tick the correct box

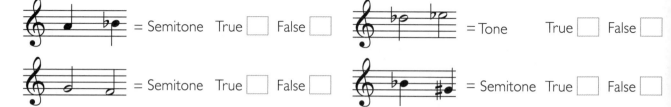

= Semitone   True ☐   False ☐

= Tone   True ☐   False ☐

= Semitone   True ☐   False ☐

= Semitone   True ☐   False ☐

3 Name the following notes, then draw and name a note a **semitone higher**. There may be more than one possible correct answer – for instance D♯ or E♭.

<u>F</u>   <u>F♯</u>   __   __   __

4 Name the following notes and then draw a note a **semitone lower**.

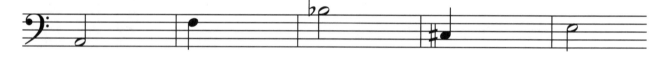

<u>E</u>   <u>E♭</u>   __   __   __

5 Name the following notes and then draw a note a **tone higher**.

<u>A</u>   <u>B</u>   __   __   __

6 Name the following notes and then draw a note a **tone lower**.

<u>E</u>   <u>D</u>   __   __   __

The Tie

A tie joins two notes of the same pitch. | See Core Book page 168.

It is specially useful for joining notes across barlines.

1 Clap the following rhythms. Watch out for those ties!

2 Musical maths! Add the tied notes together and work out the total number of beats.

Sing and Compose

Our new solfa note is **fah** – this is introduced on page 168 of the Core Book.

The following melodies are written on the stave. Work out the solfa for each melody and then sing. The small black box in front of the time signature shows which note is Doh. Use your handsigns as you sing.

Write the following melodies onto the stave and then sing them. Again, the small black box indicates Doh.

Add your own solfa to the following rhythms and then sing. Don't forget to end on Doh.

Now compose your own 4-bar rhythms. Add solfa (d, r, m, f, s, l) and sing your compositions.

The Dotted Crotchet

The dot adds half the value of the note to which it is attached. See Core Book page 169.

Clap the following rhythms.

In simple time signatures, the dotted crotchet is usually followed by a quaver.

Work out what is missing to complete the following rhythms – either a dotted crotchet or a quaver. Then clap the rhythm.

More Sing and Compose

Two More Notes

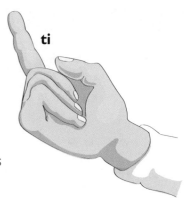

ti

Our last two solfa notes are **ti** and (high) **doh'**. High doh', written with a little dash, is an **octave** above low doh.

The following melodies are written on the stave. Work out the solfa for each melody and then sing. The small black box in front of the time signature shows which note is Doh. Use your handsigns as you sing.

Write the following melodies onto the stave and then sing them. Again, the small black box indicates Doh.

Add your own solfa to the following rhythms, ending on doh, and then sing.

Now compose your own 4-bar rhythms. Add solfa (d, r, m, f, s, l, t and d') and sing your compositions. Ti–doh is often a good way to end a melody. Don't forget to end on a long note.

The Major Scale

These two notes – ti and doh' – complete the **major scale**: see Core Book page 171. Read this page carefully to see how the major scale is built. There is always a **semitone** between **mi** and **fah**, and between **ti** and (high) **doh'**.

C, F and G Majors

1 Fill in the gaps in the major scale formula, using T or S.

T			T	T		

You can see the scale of **C major**, ascending and descending, written in the treble clef, at the bottom of Core Book page 171.

2 Write the scale of C major **ascending**, in the treble clef. Use semibreves. Add **solfa**, and circle the semitones in RED. When you write the solfa letters, remember to add a dash for high doh: d'

3 Write the scale of C major **descending**, in the treble clef. Use minims. Add **letter names**, and circle the semitones in RED.

Here is the scale of C major ascending and descending in the bass clef. It starts on the second space C and ends on middle C.

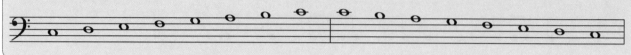

4 Write the scale of C major **ascending**, in the bass clef. Use crotchets. Add **solfa**, and circle the semitones in RED.

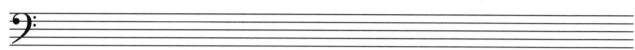

5 Write the scale of C major **descending**, in the bass clef. Use dotted minims. Add **letter names**, and circle the semitones in RED.

Look at page 172 of the Core Book to see how the tones and semitones fit in a different key: G major. **This key needs a black note, F sharp; otherwise the tones and semitones won't be right.**

6 Write the scale of G major **ascending**, in the treble clef. Use crotchets. Add **letter names**, and circle the semitones in RED. Don't forget to draw the F sharp, using a sharp sign.

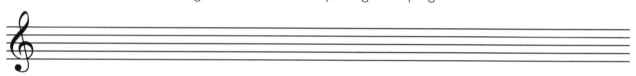

7 Write the scale of G major **descending**, in the treble clef. Use semibreves. Add **solfa**, and circle the semitones in RED.

8 Complete this scale of G major **ascending**, in the bass clef. Use minims. Add **solfa**, and circle the semitones in RED. The first four notes have been written for you.

9 Write the scale of G major **descending**, in the bass clef. Use dotted minims. Add **letter names**, and circle the semitones in RED.

Look again at page 172 of the Core Book to see how the tones and semitones fit in F major. **This key needs a different black note, B flat, to make the order of tones and semitones right.**

10 Write the scale of F major **ascending** in the treble clef. Use dotted minims. Add **solfa**, and circle the semitones in RED. Don't forget to draw the B flat, using a flat sign.

11 Write the scale of F major **descending** in the treble clef. Use crotchets. Add **solfa**, and circle the semitones in RED.

12 Complete this scale of F major **descending** in the bass clef. Use semibreves. Add **letter names**, and circle the semitones in RED. The first two and last two notes have been written for you.

13 Write the scale of F major **ascending** in the bass clef. Use crotchets. Add **letter names**, and circle the semitones in RED.

14 Fill in the blanks, giving the correct letter name.

Doh in the scale of G major =   Fah in the scale of F major =

Doh in the scale of C major =   Soh in the scale of C major =

Doh in the scale of F major =   Soh in the scale of F major =

Re in the scale of C major =   Lah in the scale of G major =

Mi in the scale of G major =   Ti in the scale of C major =

15 True or False? Are these notes the same or not?

Soh in the scale of C major = doh in the scale of G major   True   False

Doh in the scale of C major = soh in the scale of F major   True   False

Re in the scale of C major = soh in the scale of G major   True   False

Lah in the scale of F major = re in the scale of G major   True   False

Soh in the scale of G major = re in the scale of C major   True   False

Two More Major Scales: D Major and B flat Major

You can look at these on page 173 of the Core Book. They need more black notes, to get the right order of tones and semitones.

1 Write the scale of D major **ascending**, in the treble clef. Use minims. Add **letter names**, and circle the semitones in RED. **Don't forget to draw the F and C sharps.**

2 Write the scale of D major **descending**, in the treble clef. Use crotchets. Add **solfa**, and circle the semitones in RED.

3 Complete the scale of D major **ascending**, in the bass clef. Use semibreves. Add **solfa**, and circle the semitones in RED. The top note is the D above middle C, written in a ledger space.

d   r   m

4 Complete the scale of D major **descending**, in the bass clef. Use dotted minims. Add **letter names**, and circle the semitones in RED.

D   C♯

5 Complete the scale of B flat major **ascending**, in the treble clef. Use crotchets. Add **letter names**, and circle the semitones in RED.

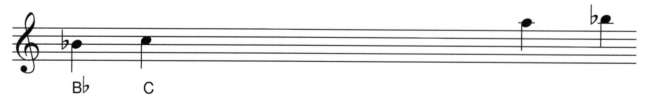

B♭   C

6 Complete the scale of B flat major **descending**, in the treble clef. Use minims. Add **solfa**, and circle the semitones in RED.

d'   t

7 Complete the scale of B flat major **ascending**, in the bass clef. Use minims. Add **solfa**, and circle the semitones in RED.

d   r

8 Name that scale! Look carefully at the sharps and flats, then name the scale (the first one has been done for you) and write all the letter names under the notes.

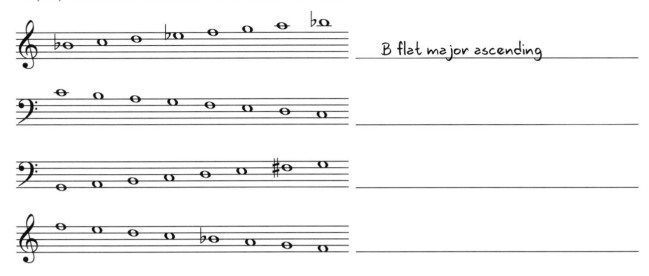

B flat major ascending

9 Add sharps or flats where needed to complete the following scales.

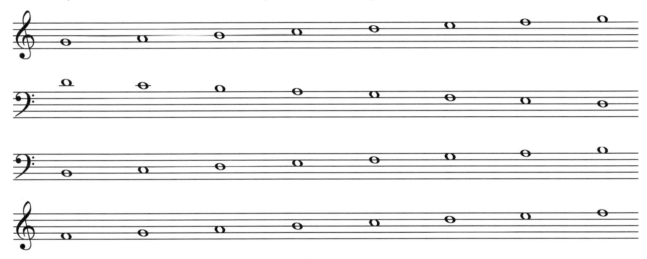

10 True or False? Are these notes the same or not?

		True	False
Soh in the scale of D major	= mi in the scale of F major	☐	☐
Re in the scale of B♭ major	= ti in the scale of D major	☐	☐
Fah in the scale of F major	= doh in the scale of B♭ major	☐	☐
Mi in the scale of D major	= doh in the scale of D major	☐	☐
Lah in the scale of B♭ major	= re in the scale of D major	☐	☐

11 Find and circle the mistakes in the following scales. Then rewrite them correctly.

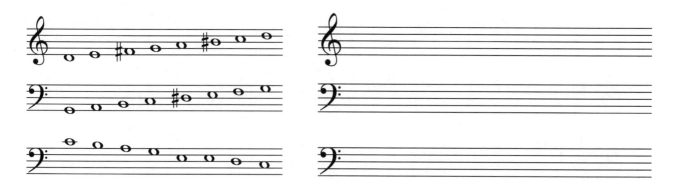

Keys and Key Signatures

These are introduced on page 174 of the Core Book. Read this page carefully, then test yourself with these exercises:

1   Look at these key signatures and name the key. (Always a major key. We'll look at minor keys in Chapter 11c.)

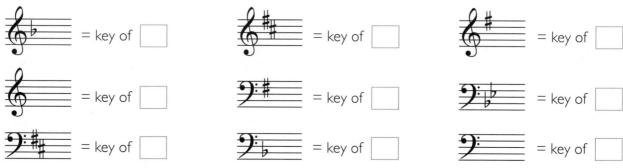

2   Draw the key signatures for the following keys:

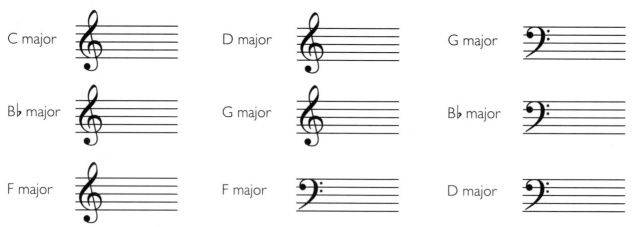

3   Look at the three melodies below. Identify the key of each melody. Then, on the blank staves, rewrite each melody **with the correct key signature**. Remember that with the key signature you won't need to write accidentals in front of the notes.

4 In a key signature, the sharps or flats must always be written on the correct line or space, and in the correct order. **The ones below have some mistakes.** Write them correctly.

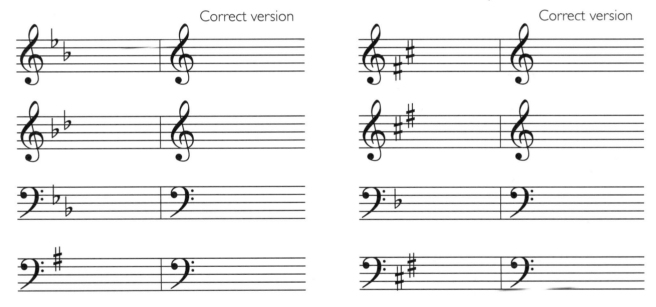

Semiquavers and Dotted Quavers

A semiquaver is half as long as a quaver. Read about semiquavers on pages 175–6 in the Core Book.

1 Clap the following rhythms.

A dotted quaver is worth one-and-a-half quavers. It often forms a pair with a semiquaver.

See Core Book page 176.

2 Clap the following rhythms.

3 True or False? Check these musical equations.

	True	False

Compound Time

In compound time, each beat is a dotted crotchet, subdivided into three quavers. The most common compound time signature is $\frac{6}{8}$, with two dotted crotchet beats in each bar. See Core Book pages 176–7.

1 Identify and circle the compound time signature in the list below.

$$\frac{4}{4} \quad \frac{6}{8} \quad \frac{3}{4} \quad \frac{2}{4}$$

2 Clap the following rhythms:

11a Composing Skills: Building Triads

Intervals

> The distance from one note to another is called an **interval**. See Core Book page 178.

1 Identify the intervals below. Remember to include the bottom and top notes as you count the number of letter names. The first four have been done for you.

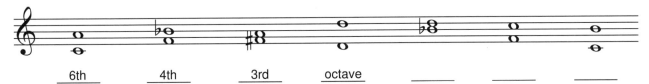

    6th   4th   3rd   octave   _____   _____   _____

   _____   _____   _____   _____   _____   _____   _____

Major and Minor 3rds

> There are different types of intervals, depending on how many semitones they contain. **Major 3rds** have four semitones; **minor 3rds** have three semitones.

See Core Book page 179. This is easier to understand if you try them out on a keyboard, or look at the keyboard diagram on page 167 of the Core Book.

2 Look at the 3rds below. Count the semitones, and say whether they are major or minor.

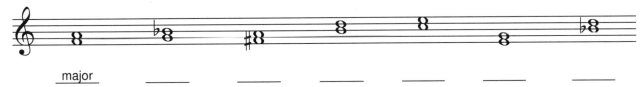

    major   _____   _____   _____   _____   _____

3 Here are some more, this time in the bass clef.

   _____   _____   _____   _____   _____   _____

4 Which note is a major 3rd above C? _____

   Which note is a minor 3rd above C? _____

   Add these two notes on the stave below:

       major 3rd   minor 3rd

Triads

Triads are three-note chords, consisting of:

- the root note
- the 3rd above the root
- the 5th above the root

See Core Book page 179.

Triads can be major or minor. A **major triad** has a **major 3rd** from the root to the middle note, and then a **minor 3rd** from there to the top note. A **minor triad** has a **minor 3rd** from the root to the middle note, and then a **major 3rd** from there to the top note. This is explained on Core Book page 180. Again, it helps if you can play the examples on a keyboard, or use a keyboard diagram to count the intervals.

1 Are these triads major or minor? Look carefully at the interval from the root note. The first four have been done for you. The last four are in the bass clef.

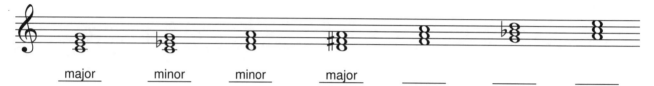

   major   minor   minor   major

2 Name these triads. Use the name of the root note, then whether it is major or minor.

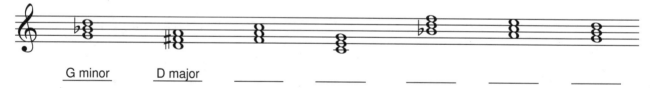

   G minor   D major

3 Write these triads on the stave.

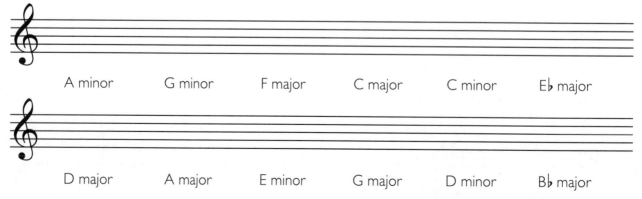

A minor   G minor   F major   C major   C minor   E♭ major

D major   A major   E minor   G major   D minor   B♭ major

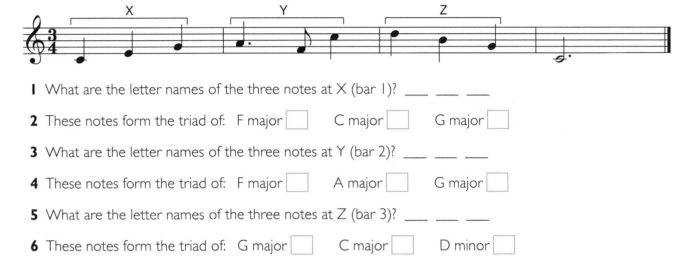

| G major | A major | G minor | C major | D minor | F major |

Triads in Melodies

Look at the following 4-bar melody and answer the questions.

Check the key signature and work out the key before you start.

1 What are the letter names of the three notes at X (bar 1)? ___ ___ ___

2 These notes form the triad of: F major ☐ C major ☐ G major ☐

3 What are the letter names of the three notes at Y (bar 2)? ___ ___ ___

4 These notes form the triad of: F major ☐ A major ☐ G major ☐

5 What are the letter names of the three notes at Z (bar 3)? ___ ___ ___

6 These notes form the triad of: G major ☐ C major ☐ D minor ☐

Inversions

> If the root of a triad is moved up an octave, and the 3rd or 5th is placed at the bottom, the chord is **inverted**.

See Core Book page 181, Jumbled Triads.

1 Identify these inverted chords. They are all major chords.

G major   D major   _____   _____   _____   _____

2 Identify these inverted chords. Some are major and some are minor.

_____   _____   _____   _____   _____   _____

3 Re-arrange these inverted triads, re-writing them in their root position, and name the chord.

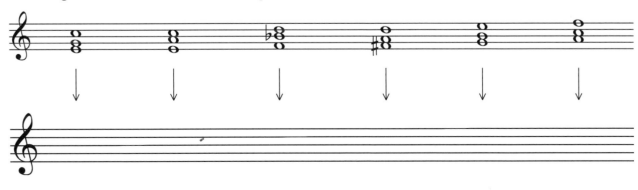

_____   _____   _____   _____   _____   _____

More Triads in Melodies

Look at the following 4-bar melodies and answer the questions.

Check the key signature and work out the key before you start.

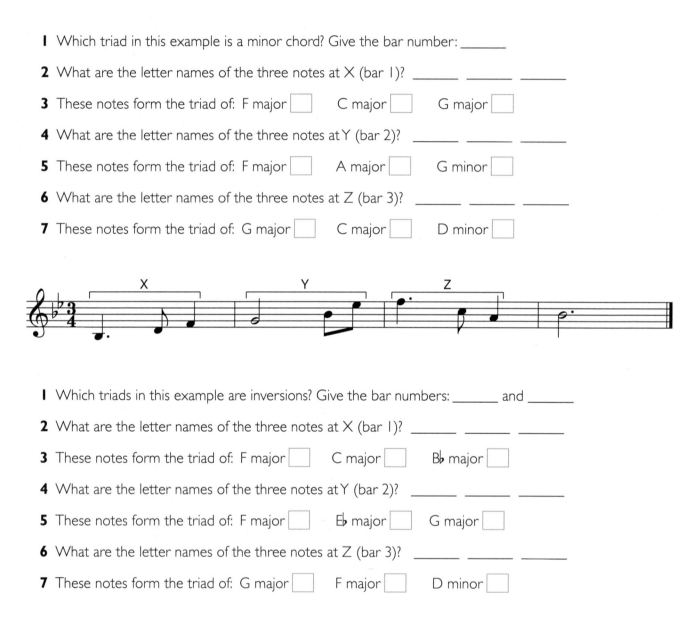

1 Which triad in this example is a minor chord? Give the bar number: _____

2 What are the letter names of the three notes at X (bar 1)? _____ _____ _____

3 These notes form the triad of: F major ☐ C major ☐ G major ☐

4 What are the letter names of the three notes at Y (bar 2)? _____ _____ _____

5 These notes form the triad of: F major ☐ A major ☐ G minor ☐

6 What are the letter names of the three notes at Z (bar 3)? _____ _____ _____

7 These notes form the triad of: G major ☐ C major ☐ D minor ☐

1 Which triads in this example are inversions? Give the bar numbers: _____ and _____

2 What are the letter names of the three notes at X (bar 1)? _____ _____ _____

3 These notes form the triad of: F major ☐ C major ☐ B♭ major ☐

4 What are the letter names of the three notes at Y (bar 2)? _____ _____ _____

5 These notes form the triad of: F major ☐ E♭ major ☐ G major ☐

6 What are the letter names of the three notes at Z (bar 3)? _____ _____ _____

7 These notes form the triad of: G major ☐ F major ☐ D minor ☐

Unessential Notes

> Unessential notes decorate the melody. They may be passing notes, lower auxiliary notes or upper auxiliary notes.

See Core Book pages 181–2.

Circle and label the unessential notes in each of the following bars.

Exam-style Triad Questions

Turn the Glasses Over

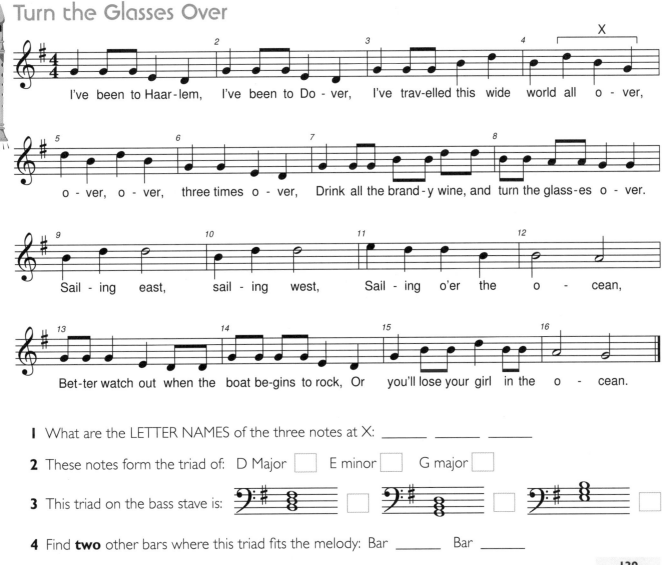

1 What are the LETTER NAMES of the three notes at X: _____ _____ _____

2 These notes form the triad of: D Major ☐   E minor ☐   G major ☐

3 This triad on the bass stave is: [notation] ☐   [notation] ☐   [notation] ☐

4 Find **two** other bars where this triad fits the melody: Bar _____   Bar _____

Morning Has Broken

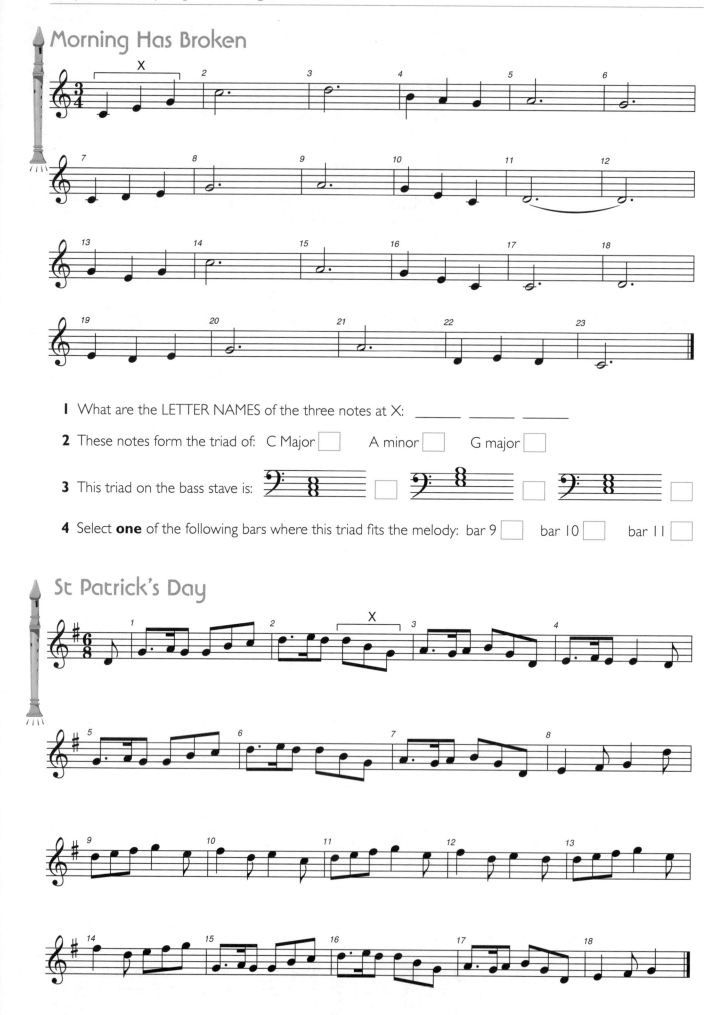

1 What are the LETTER NAMES of the three notes at X: _____ _____ _____

2 These notes form the triad of: C Major ☐   A minor ☐   G major ☐

3 This triad on the bass stave is: [bass clef triad] ☐   [bass clef triad] ☐   [bass clef triad] ☐

4 Select **one** of the following bars where this triad fits the melody: bar 9 ☐   bar 10 ☐   bar 11 ☐

St Patrick's Day

1 What are the LETTER NAMES of the three notes at X: _____ _____ _____

2 These notes form the triad of: D Major ☐   A minor ☐   G major ☐

3 This triad on the bass stave is: ☐ ☐ ☐

4 Select **one** of the following places where this triad fits the melody:

first half of bar 4 ☐   2nd half of bar 10 ☐   2nd half of bar 17 ☐

Theme from the New World Symphony

Dvořák

1 What are the LETTER NAMES of the four notes at X (bar 1)?

Note 1: _____   Note 2: _____   Note 3: _____   Note 4: _____

2 Three of these notes form the triad of: G major ☐   A major ☐   D major ☐   D minor ☐

3 This triad on the bass stave is: ☐ ☐ ☐

4 Select ONE other bar where the same triad would fit the melody:

Bar 5 ☐   Bar 8 ☐   Bar 14 ☐   Bar 15 ☐

5 Which of the four notes at X is an unessential note? _____

11b Chord Progressions

The exam question on chord progressions only needs to be answered at Higher Level.

Degrees of the Scale

Each degree of the scale has a name, as well as its solfa name, starting with **tonic** for Doh. See Core Book page 178.

1 Label the missing degrees of the scale.

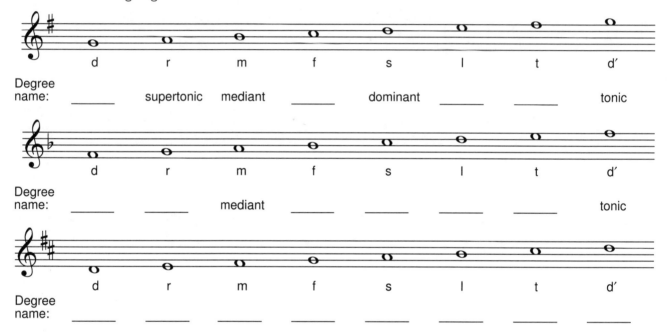

Triads Built on the Scale

A triad can be built on every note of the scale.

The Core Book page 179 shows how this works in C major.

1 Write a series of triads built on a D major scale. The first two have been done for you.

2 Do the same in F major. This time no help has been given, so you must start by writing the correct key signature for F major, then the chords.

Naming Triads

> The triad can be named after its root note, using its solfa name (for instance 'doh chord' or 'doh triad') or the name of the degree of the scale (for instance 'tonic chord').
>
> The degrees of the scale are also numbered, using Roman numerals, and this is another way of naming the chords. Lower-case (small) letters are used for minor chords, for instance ii instead of II.
>
> Only chords I, ii, IV, V and vi are used at Junior Certificate.

3 Complete this chart of chords in C major. Under the notes, write in the missing degrees of the scale. Below that, for each chord write whether it is major or minor. (Look carefully at what notes are in the chord, counting the semitones to work out the intervals.) Below that, write the correct Roman numerals, using small letters for the minor chords.

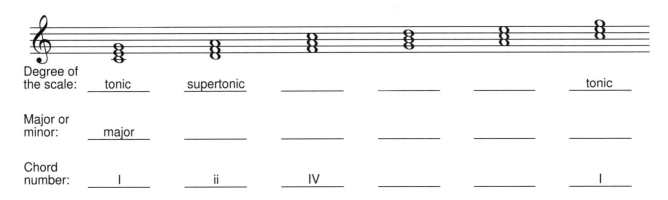

Degree of the scale:	tonic	supertonic	_____	_____	_____	tonic
Major or minor:	major	_____	_____	_____	_____	_____
Chord number:	I	ii	IV	_____	_____	I

4 In the same way, complete this chart of chords in F major.

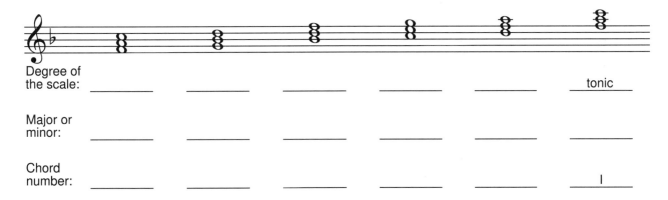

Degree of the scale:	_____	_____	_____	_____	_____	tonic
Major or minor:	_____	_____	_____	_____	_____	_____
Chord number:	_____	_____	_____	_____	_____	I

5 All major scales share the same pattern of intervals and chords. Which three degrees of the major scale have major triads?

_____ _____ _____

Chord Symbols

Chords can also be named after the root (bottom note). Chord symbols are a short form of these names: **C** for C major and **Cm** for C minor.

Name the triads in the five exercises below, filling in all the gaps with the **chord symbols**, the **solfa names** and the **Roman numerals**. Remember to check the key signature. (Watch out for the flats, especially in B♭ major.)

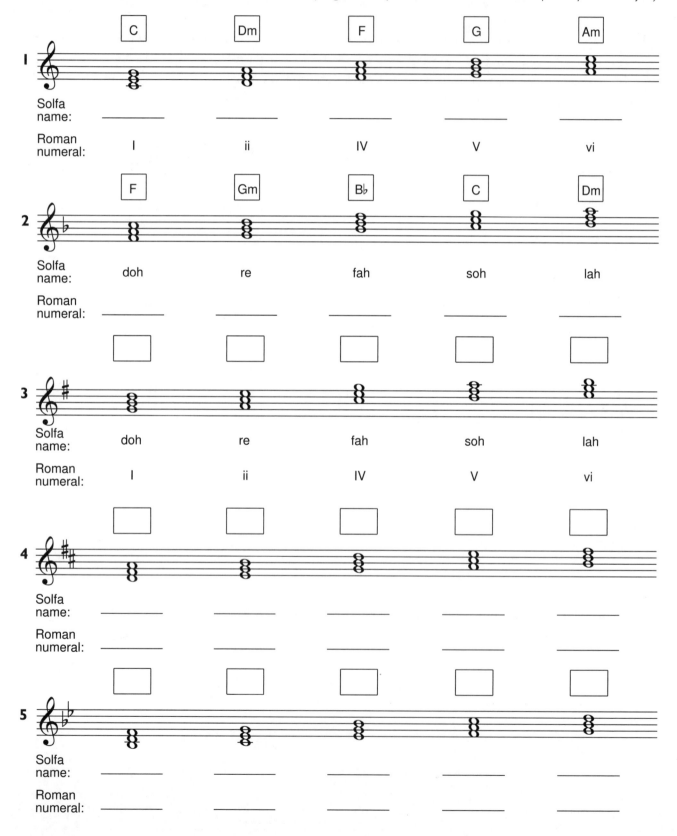

I, IV and V

> These three chords – **tonic**, **subdominant** and **dominant** – are specially important in chord progressions. You need to learn them in each of the keys you use for Junior Certificate.

1 Go back to the last five exercises. Circle and label the tonic, subdominant and dominant chords.

2 Name and then draw the following triads.

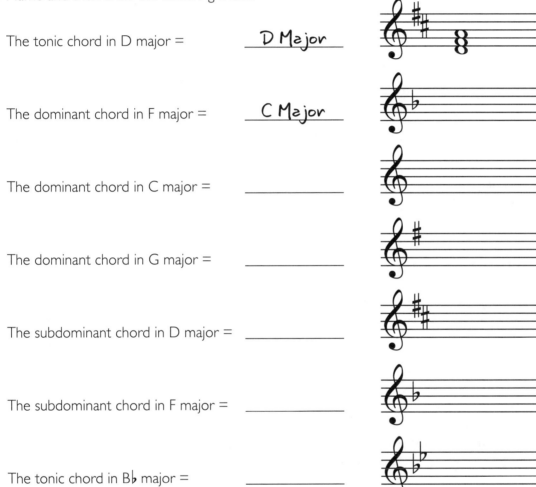

The tonic chord in D major =   D Major

The dominant chord in F major =   C Major

The dominant chord in C major =   _____

The dominant chord in G major =   _____

The subdominant chord in D major =   _____

The subdominant chord in F major =   _____

The tonic chord in B♭ major =   _____

Backing Chords Using I, IV and V

Read about backing chords on Core Book page 183.

Look carefully at the following simple melodies.

Add chord symbols, choosing chords that share the same notes as the melody.

Here is one that has been done for you. Look at the melody notes, and you will see that the chosen chord has the same notes. Remember that each chord lasts until the next chord box.

Remember also that the chord notes in the melody are not necessarily in root position. They may be **inversions**, as in bars 2 and 3 below.

Now choose your own backing chords for the next four melodies. Use the **root name** of the chord, not Roman numerals. Do NOT have the same symbol twice in succession. Remember to check the key signature. Watch out for unessential notes in the melody.

The Dominant Seventh Chord (V7)

We can add another note to a triad, a 7th above the root note. The most common chord to have the seventh added is the **dominant** (soh) triad, and the result is called a **dominant seventh** chord – see Core Book page 184. It is very useful because it leads naturally to the tonic chord.

The chord symbol for a dominant seventh chord is the root note plus the number 7. For example, in the **key of C major** the dominant note is **G** (the fifth note of the scale), the dominant triad is **G major**, and the dominant seventh is a **G7** chord.

Write out the following dominant seventh chords and their chord symbols. The first one has been done for you.

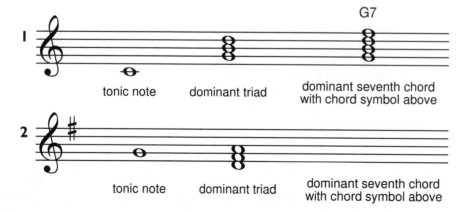

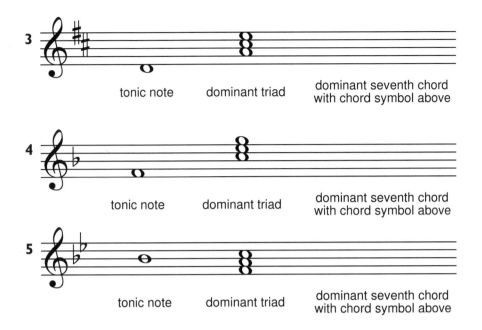

3

tonic note   dominant triad   dominant seventh chord with chord symbol above

4

tonic note   dominant triad   dominant seventh chord with chord symbol above

5

tonic note   dominant triad   dominant seventh chord with chord symbol above

Backing Chords Including a Dominant Seventh Chord

Look at this melody, and add chord symbols. In which bar do the melody notes form a dominant seventh chord?

6

Cadences

Make sure you understand the four types of cadence, as explained in the Core Book (pages 185–7).

Complete the following **Cadence Grid** – the first one has been filled in for you.

Cadence	Chords	Key of C major	Key of G major	Key of F major	Key of D major	Key of B♭ major
Perfect	V–I / Soh–Doh	G–C	D–G	C–F	A–D	F–B♭
Plagal						
Imperfect						
Interrupted						

True or False?

1 I–V = Perfect Cadence   True ☐   False ☐

2 IV–I = Plagal Cadence   True ☐   False ☐

3 ii–V = Interrupted Cadence   True ☐   False ☐

4 V–I = Perfect Cadence   True ☐   False ☐

5 False Cadence = V–vi   True ☐   False ☐

6 IV–V = Perfect Cadence   True ☐   False ☐

7 V–vi = Interrupted Cadence   True ☐   False ☐

8 Amen Cadence = IV–I   True ☐   False ☐

Approaching Cadences: Good Chord Progressions

Approach chords are discussed on Core Book pages 186–7.

Fill in the blanks in the questions below. Choose a good approach chord for the first blank, then name the cadence in the second one. You can use solfa or Roman numerals.

1 _____–soh–doh = a _____ cadence   **4** _____–re–soh = a _____ cadence

_____–V–I = a _____ cadence   _____–ii–V = a _____ cadence

2 _____–fah–doh = a _____ cadence   **5** _____–V–vi = a _____ cadence

_____–IV–I = a _____ cadence   _____–soh–lah = a _____ cadence

3 _____–fah–soh = a _____ cadence

_____–IV–V = a _____ cadence

Backing Chords Questions

Add chordal accompaniments to the following melodies by selecting suitable backing chords.

- It's a good idea to identify the **key** and sketch a chord plan first.
- Select the most suitable chord for each chord box. Use **chord symbols** (root names), not Roman numerals or solfa.
- Do not have the same chord symbol twice in succession.
- Remember, for all **minor chords** the chord symbol must include a small 'm'.
- Watch out for **unessential** notes, and for chord notes in **inversions**.
- Don't forget to have a **perfect** or **plagal** cadence to end.

Did you ever see a lassie?

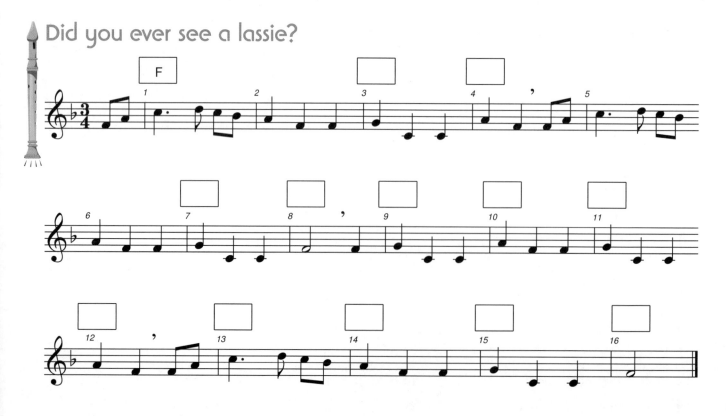

Les Bouffons

Amazing Grace

Little Donkey

Jesse James

Curly Locks

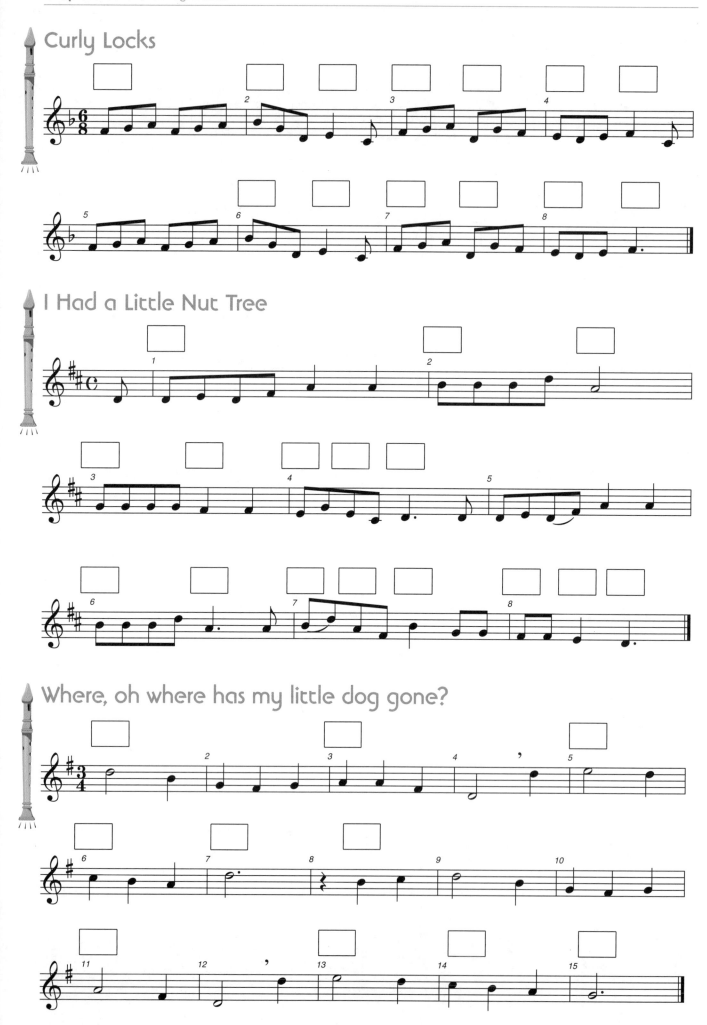

I Had a Little Nut Tree

Where, oh where has my little dog gone?

Portsmouth

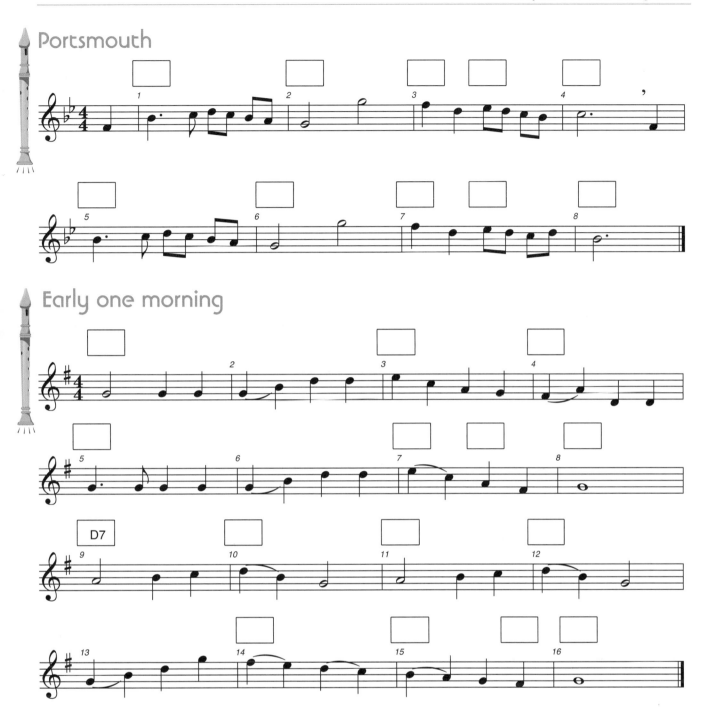

Early one morning

As you will notice, we have suggested a dominant seventh for one of the chords. When you are writing backing chords, dominant sevenths can be very useful.

Goosey, Goosey Gander

Father O'Flynn

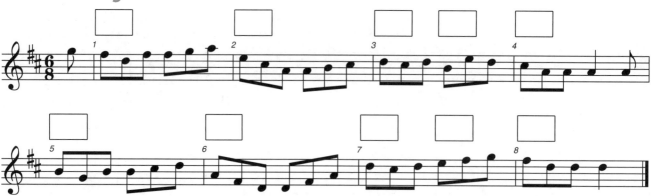

Cadence Questions

In the exam, for question 8 you choose between two types of **cadence** question or a **backing chords** question. The two types of cadence question are:

A – Add melody and bass notes at cadences for keyboard.

      OR

B – Add chords at cadences for SATB choir.

Adding Notes to a Bass Line

Add melody notes to the following cadences.

      OR

Add soprano, alto and tenor parts to the following cadences.

Then name the cadence.

Remember to check the key signature in each exercise.

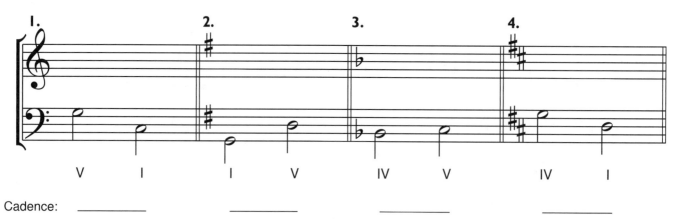

Cadence: _____   _____   _____   _____

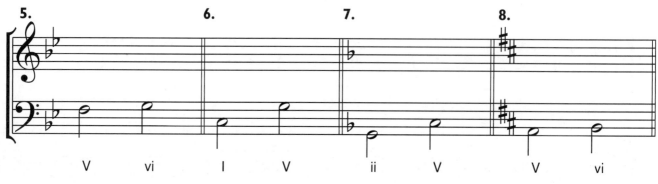

Cadence: _____   _____   _____   _____

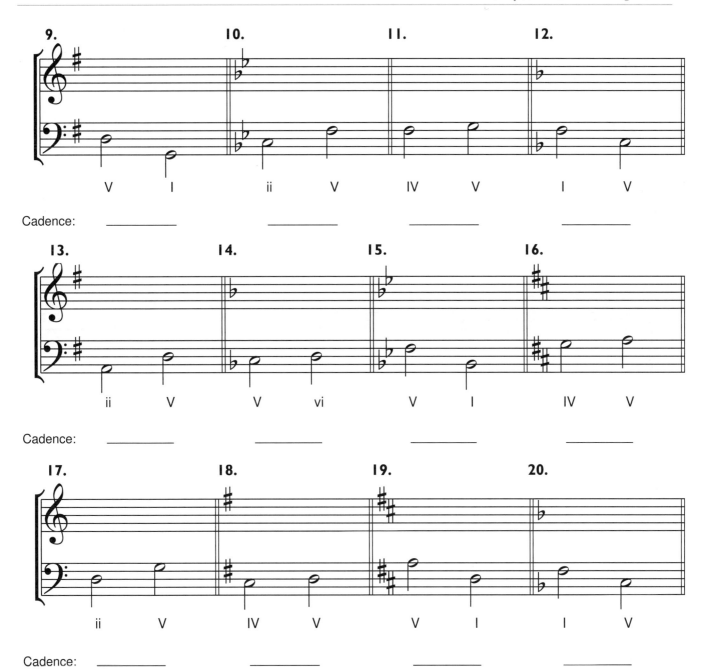

Cadence: _____   _____   _____   _____

Adding Notes to a Melody Line

Add bass notes to the following cadences.

OR

Add alto, tenor and bass parts to the following cadences.

Then name the cadence.

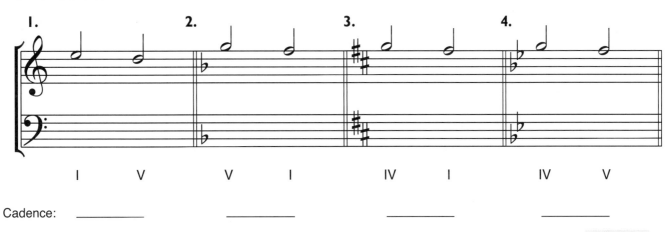

Cadence: _____   _____   _____   _____

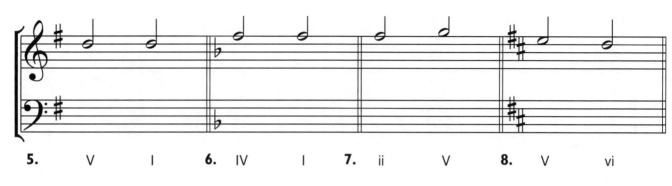

5.　　　V　　　I　　　6. IV　　　I　　　7. ii　　　V　　　8. V　　　vi

Cadence: _____　　_____　　_____　　_____

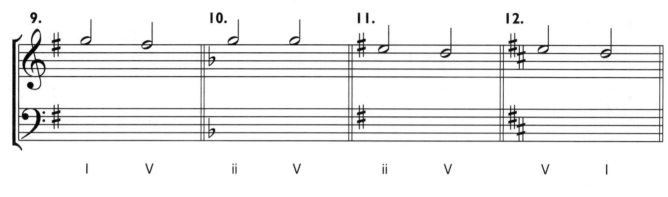

9.　　　　10.　　　　11.　　　　12.

I　　　V　　　ii　　　V　　　ii　　　V　　　V　　　I

Cadence: _____　　_____　　_____　　_____

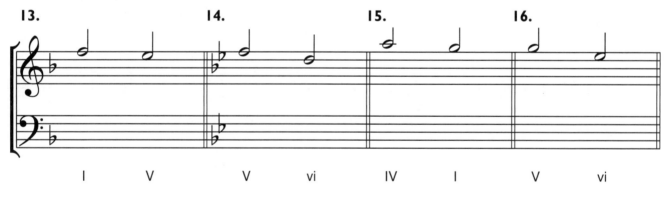

13.　　　　14.　　　　15.　　　　16.

I　　　V　　　V　　　vi　　　IV　　　I　　　V　　　vi

Cadence: _____　　_____　　_____　　_____

17.　　　　18.　　　　19.　　　　20.

IV　　　I　　　I　　　V　　　V　　　I　　　V　　　vi

Cadence: _____　　_____　　_____　　_____

Cadences with Approach Chords — Adding to a Bass Line

Add melody notes to the following chord progressions.

OR

Add soprano, alto and tenor parts to the following chord progressions.

Then name the cadence formed by the final two chords of each progression.

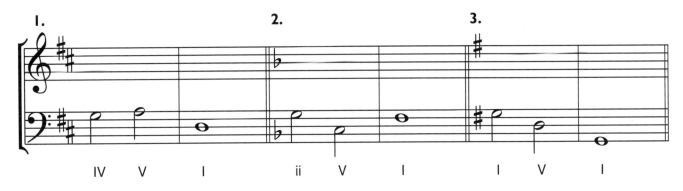

Cadence: _____   _____   _____

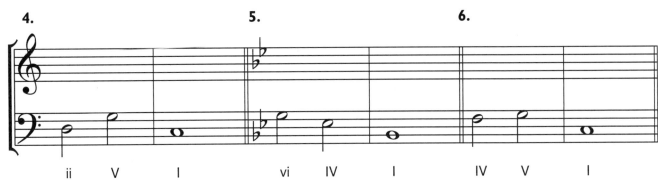

Cadence: _____   _____   _____

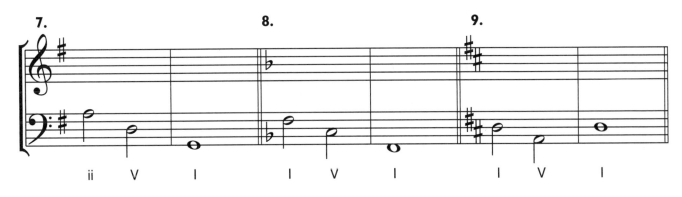

Cadence: _____   _____   _____

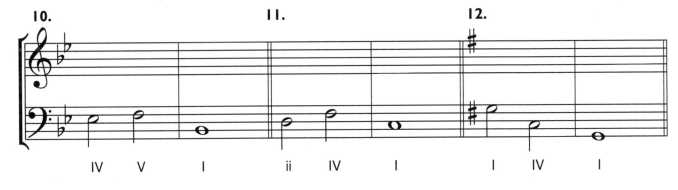

Cadence: _____   _____   _____

Cadences with Approach Chords — Adding to a Melody Line

Add bass notes to the following chord progressions.

OR

Add alto, tenor and bass parts to the following chord progressions.
Name the cadence formed by the final two chords of each progression.

Cadence: _____   _____   _____

Cadence: _____   _____   _____

Cadence: _____   _____   _____

Cadence: _____   _____   _____

Exam-type Questions

Option A — Add Melody and Bass Notes at Cadences for Keyboard

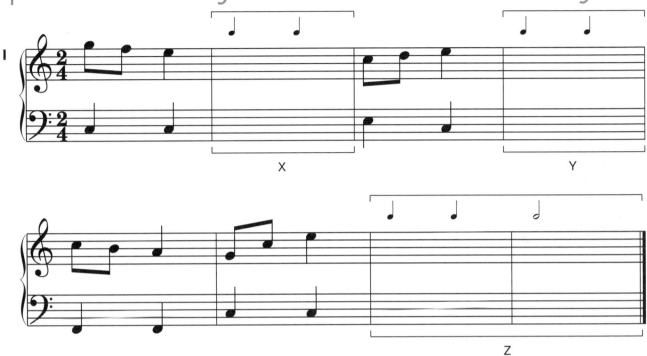

Add melody and bass notes to form the following:

(i) At X an IMPERFECT cadence (ii–V)

(ii) At Y an INTERRUPTED cadence (V–vi)

(iii) At Z a PERFECT cadence and its approach chord (IV–V–I)

Add melody and bass notes to form the following:

(i) At X an INTERRUPTED cadence (V–vi)

(ii) At Y an IMPERFECT cadence (IV–V)

(iii) At Z a PERFECT cadence and its approach chord (ii–V–I)

Add melody and bass notes to form the following:

  (i) At X a PLAGAL cadence (IV–I)

 (ii) At Y an INTERRUPTED cadence (V–vi)

(iii) At Z a PERFECT cadence and its approach chord (IV–V–I)

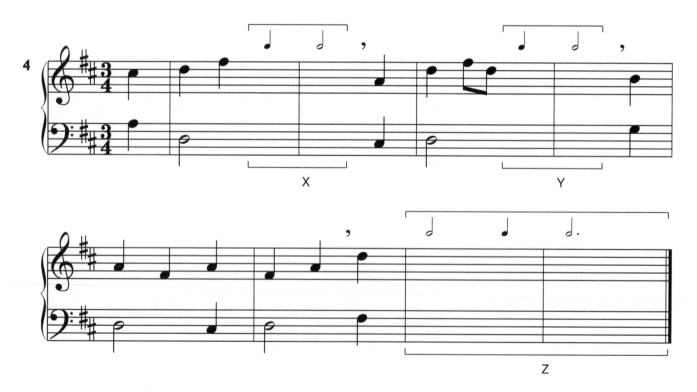

Add melody and bass notes to form the following:

  (i) At X an IMPERFECT cadence (IV–V)

 (ii) At Y an INTERRUPTED cadence (V–vi)

(iii) At Z a PERFECT cadence and its approach chord (ii–V–I)

Add melody and bass notes to form the following:

(i) At X an INTERRUPTED cadence (V–vi)

(ii) At Y an IMPERFECT cadence (ii–V)

(iii) At Z a PERFECT cadence and its approach chord (IV–V–I)

Add melody and bass notes to form the following:

(i) At X an IMPERFECT cadence (ii–V)

(ii) At Y an INTERRUPTED cadence (V–vi)

(iii) At Z a PLAGAL cadence and its approach chord (I–IV–I)

Option B — Compose Chords at Cadences for SATB Choir

Add three or four voices as appropriate to form the following cadences:

(i) At X an IMPERFECT cadence (IV–V)

(ii) At Y an INTERRUPTED cadence (V–vi)

(iii) At Z a PERFECT cadence (ii–V–I)

Add three or four voices as appropriate to form the following cadences:

(i) At X an INTERRUPTED cadence (V–vi)

(ii) At Y an IMPERFECT cadence (IV–V)

(iii) At Z a PERFECT cadence (IV–V–I)

Add three or four voices as appropriate to form the following cadences:

(i) At X a PLAGAL cadence (IV–I)

(ii) At Y an IMPERFECT cadence (ii–V)

(iii) At Z a PERFECT cadence (IV–V–I)

Add three or four voices as appropriate to form the following cadences:

(i) At X an IMPERFECT cadence (ii–V)

(ii) At Y an INTERRUPTED cadence (V–vi)

(iii) At Z a PLAGAL cadence (I–IV–I)

Minor Scales

> To find the **relative minor** of a major scale, start on the sixth degree (lah) of the major scale. See Core Book pages 190–91.
>
> In a **harmonic minor** scale the seventh note is sharpened, using an **accidental**. See Core Book pages 192–3.

1 Write out the relative harmonic minor of C major.

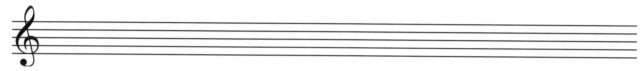

2 Write out the relative harmonic minor of G major.

3 Write out the relative harmonic minor of F major.

4 Sing and identify the key of the following two melodies:

(a)

(b)

5 Identify the key of the following two melodies, then sharpen the 7th, using an accidental, then SING.

(a)

(b)

Triads in Minor Keys

Triads in minor keys are discussed on Core Book page 194. In minor keys, the triads you need for Junior Certificate are:

- i   tonic
- iv subdominant
- V   dominant
- VI submediant

Two of these are major chords and two are minor. Look at the example at the top of Core Book page 194 to see which are which.

This is the same for all minor keys, because the pattern of major and minor intervals is always the same.

Triads in Melodies

Look at the two 4-bar melodies below and answer the questions below.

Check the key signature and work out the key before you start.

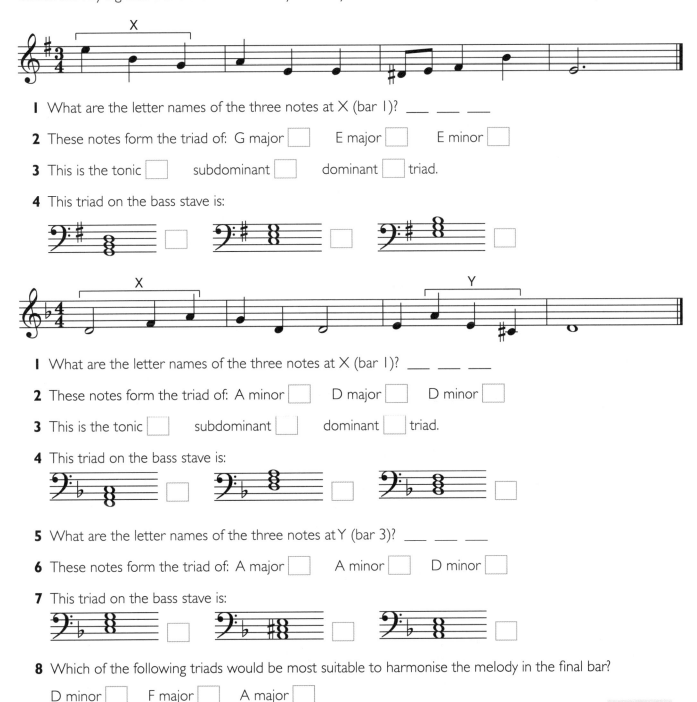

1 What are the letter names of the three notes at X (bar 1)? ___ ___ ___

2 These notes form the triad of: G major ☐   E major ☐   E minor ☐

3 This is the tonic ☐   subdominant ☐   dominant ☐ triad.

4 This triad on the bass stave is:

1 What are the letter names of the three notes at X (bar 1)? ___ ___ ___

2 These notes form the triad of: A minor ☐   D major ☐   D minor ☐

3 This is the tonic ☐   subdominant ☐   dominant ☐ triad.

4 This triad on the bass stave is:

5 What are the letter names of the three notes at Y (bar 3)? ___ ___ ___

6 These notes form the triad of: A major ☐   A minor ☐   D minor ☐

7 This triad on the bass stave is:

8 Which of the following triads would be most suitable to harmonise the melody in the final bar?

D minor ☐   F major ☐   A major ☐

Exam-type Triad Questions

Look at the following melody and answer the questions below.

Check the key signature and work out the key before you start.

River Wisla

Polish folk song

1 What are the letter names of the three notes at X (bar 5)? ___ ___ ___

2 These notes form the triad of: D minor ☐   C major ☐   A minor ☐   D major ☐

3 This triad on the bass stave is:

4 In which of the following bars does this triad fit the melody?

bar 2 ☐   bar 8 ☐   bar 9 ☐   bar 12 ☐

5 What are the letter names of the three notes at Y (bar 9)? ___ ___ ___

6 These notes form the triad of: A minor ☐   E minor ☐   E major ☐   C major ☐

7 This triad on the bass stave is:

8 In which of the following bars does this triad fit the melody?

bar 6 ☐   bar 10 ☐   bar 13 ☐   bar 14 ☐

9 This is the tonic ☐   subdominant ☐   dominant ☐ triad.

Backing Chords in Minor Keys

Look carefully at the following short melodies, and add chord symbols, choosing chords that share the same notes as the melody.

- Start by looking at the key signature and identifying the key.
- Remember that the chord notes in the melody are not necessarily in root position. They may be **inversions**.
- Use the root name of the chord, not Roman numerals.

Do not have the same symbol twice in succession.

6 Add a chordal accompaniment to the following melody by selecting suitable backing chords.

The Knight's Song

Cadences and Chord Progressions in Minor Keys

These exercises are like the ones in Chapter 11b, except that they are in minor keys. Don't forget to sharpen the leading note, so that chord V, the dominant chord, becomes a major chord.

Add melody notes to the following cadences.

OR

Add soprano, alto and tenor parts to the following cadences.

Then name the cadence. Remember to check the key signature in each exercise.

Add bass notes to the following cadences.

OR

Add alto, tenor and bass parts to the following cadences.

Then name the cadence.

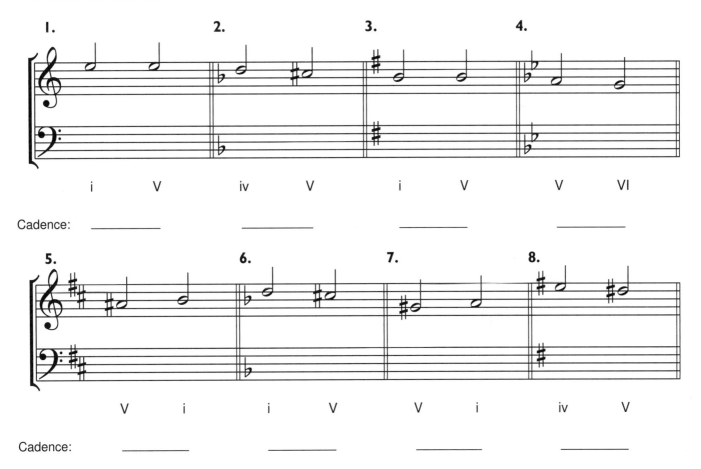

Cadence: _____ _____ _____ _____

Cadence: _____ _____ _____ _____

Cadences with Approach Chords — Adding to a Bass Line

Add melody notes to the following chord progressions.

OR

Add soprano, alto and tenor parts to the following chord progressions.

Then name the cadence formed by the final two chords of each progression.

Cadence: _____ _____ _____

Cadences with Approach Chords — Adding to a Melody Line

Add bass notes to the following chord progressions.

OR

Add alto, tenor and bass parts to the following chord progressions.

Name the cadence formed by the final two chords of each progression.

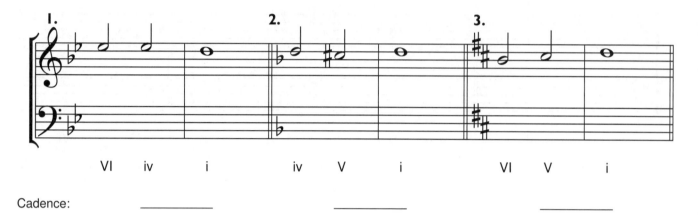

Cadence: _____   _____   _____

Exam-type Questions

Option A — Add Melody and Bass Notes at Cadences for Keyboard

Add melody and bass notes to form the following:

(i) At X an IMPERFECT cadence (i–V)

(ii) At Y an INTERRUPTED cadence (V–VI)

(iii) At Z a PERFECT cadence and its approach chord (iv–V–i)

Option B — Compose Chords at Cadences for SATB Choir

Add three or four voices as appropriate to form the following cadences:

(i) At X an IMPERFECT cadence (i–V)

(ii) At Y an INTERRUPTED cadence (V–VI)

(iii) At Z a PERFECT cadence (iv–V–i)

Melody Writing in Minor Keys

Question 7 in the Junior Certificate exam is melody writing, and is usually in a major key. The next chapter in the Workbook, Chapter 12a, gives you lots of exercises to prepare for this question.

However, it is useful to be able to write in minor keys as well because it can give your songs and tunes a bigger range of expression – so we include some melody-writing exercises in minor keys here. You should do Chapter 12a first, then come back to these.

Recognising Minor Keys

When you look at a question in the exam, it is important to realise whether you are in a major or minor key. It will probably be major, but could be minor.

- Look at the key signature first.
- Look at the first note. It is often the keynote.
- Try to hear the notes in your head.
- If there are accidentals, this may indicate a minor key, because the leading note (the 7th degree of the scale) is often sharpened.

Exercise: Compose a Melody to a Given Rhythm

Compose a melody in D minor to this four-bar rhythm. Make sure you end on the keynote or Lah. Add suitable phrasing.

Composing a Phrase set to a Given Text

The first two lines of the following stanza have been set to music. Compose your own four-bar answering phrase to complete the melody. Follow these guidelines:

- You are given the rhythm of the opening lines, but it's a good idea to write out each line and separate words of two or more syllables.
- Speak through the stanza and draw a barline before the accented syllables.
- Write out a rhythm pattern to match the words.
- Sing the opening phrase, as it will 'inspire' your answering phrase.
- The mood should reflect the words of the poem.
- Remember to end on the keynote.
- Make sure you write the words or syllables underneath the correct notes.
- See Core Book pages 202–3 for some examples and more advice.

The goblins prowl, the dogs will howl
And spooky things are seen;
A witch in flight, the moon is bright,
Tonight is Halloween.   **Anonymous**

Composing a Phrase set to a Given Opening

You are given the first bar of a four-bar melody. You must add three more bars to make a complete phrase. Follow these guidelines:

- Start by adding three bars to the rhythm pattern. Remember, it's a good idea to end on a long note.
- Then compose a melody for your rhythm. Use the given key, and end on the keynote.

Add suitable phrasing.

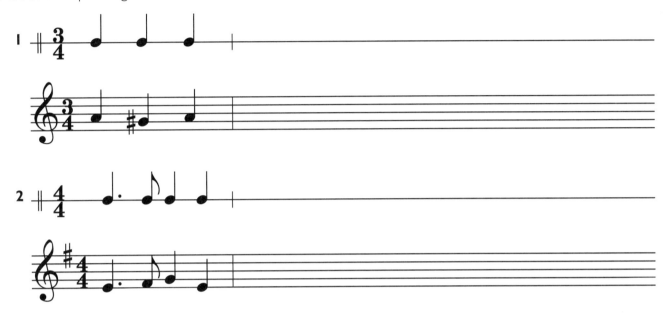

Composing an Answering Phrase

You are given a four-bar melodic phrase. You must compose an answering phrase. Follow these guidelines:

- Look closely at the given opening phrase before starting on the answering phrase.
- Start by getting organised – identify the key and write out the scale.
- Compose the rhythm of your answering phrase. Remember to end on a long note.
- End on the keynote, lah.
- Add suitable phrasing.

Given opening phrase

Rhythm of answering phrase

Finished answering phrase

Composing a Phrase Using a Given Rhythm

See Chapter 12 in Core Book for some helpful hints.

Compose your own melodies to the four-bar rhythms below. Follow these guidelines:

- Look carefully at the rhythm and make sure you know how it goes.
- Take note of the key you are asked to use.
- End on the keynote (**doh**).
- Add suitable phrasing.

1 Write a four-bar melody in **C major**, using this rhythm:

2 Write a four-bar melody in **G major**, using this rhythm:

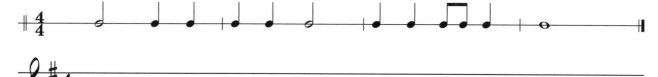

3 Write a four-bar melody in **F major,** using this rhythm:

4 Write a four-bar melody in **C major**, using this rhythm:

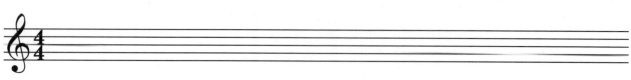

5 Write a four-bar melody in **F major**, using this rhythm:

6 Write a four-bar melody in **C major,** using this rhythm:

7 Write a four-bar melody in **D major,** using this rhythm:

8 Write a four-bar melody in **F major**, using this rhythm:

9 Write a four-bar melody in **B♭ major**, using this rhythm:

10 Write a four-bar melody in **D major**, using this rhythm:

Composing a Phrase Set to a Given Text

See Core Book pages 202–3 for help with this. You are given four lines of a poem. The first two lines have already been set to music, and you must set the remaining words, composing your own four-bar answering phrase to complete the melody. Follow these guidelines:

- Look carefully at what has already been written, and make sure you know how it goes.
- Write a four-bar rhythm to match the remaining words. Make sure you end on a long note. (Why do you think that would sound best?)
- Compose a suitable melody. Use the same key as the given opening.
- End on the keynote, doh.
- Insert the words or syllables underneath the notes.
- Add suitable phrasing.

I *Who has seen the wind?*
Neither you nor I:
But when the trees bow down their heads
The wind is passing by. Christina Rossetti

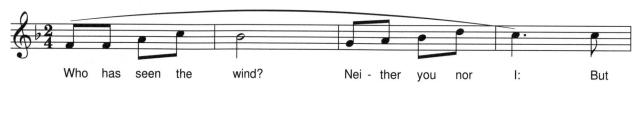

2 *I am extremely musical,*
My voice is quite sublime.
I sing sweeter than a nightingale,
No voice compares to mine. Gervase Phinn

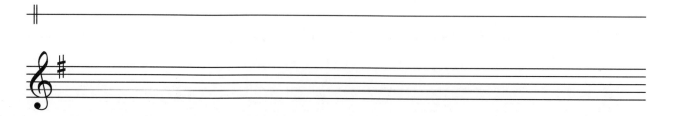

3 *I wish I were a crotchet,*
I'd sing and dance and play
Among the dotted minims
All the living day Roger McGough

4 *I must go down to the seas again,*
To the lonely sea and the sky,
And all I ask is a tall ship
And a star to steer her by John Masefield

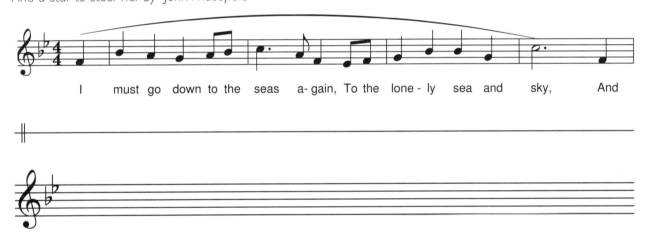

Composing a Phrase Set to a Given Opening

See Core Book pages 196–9. For this question, you are given the first bar of a four-bar melody. You must add three more bars to make a complete phrase. Follow these guidelines:

- Start by adding three bars to the rhythm pattern. Remember, it's a good idea to end on a long note.
- Then compose a melody for your rhythm. Use the given key, and end on doh.
- Add suitable phrasing.

Composing an Answering Phrase

See Core Book pages 199–201. For this question, you are given a four-bar melodic phrase. You must compose an answering phrase. Follow these guidelines:

- Look closely at the given opening phrase before starting on the answering phrase.
- Start by getting organised – identify the key and write out the scale.
- Firstly you should compose the rhythm of your answering phrase. Remember to end on a long note.
- Then think about the melody. End on the keynote, doh.
- Add suitable phrasing.

1 Given opening phrase

Rhythm of answering phrase

Finished answering phrase

Melody Writing in Minor Keys

There are some melody-writing exercises using minor keys at the end of Chapter 11c, pages 169–171.

It is useful to be able to write in minor keys as well as major, and important to recognise minor keys in an exam question. Chapter 11c will help you with this.

12b | Composing Skills: Free Composition

Free Composition is question 9 in the Junior Certificate examination (Higher Level only), and is an alternative to questions 6, 7 and 8 combined. It needs a high degree of accomplishment, so consult your teacher before attempting this question.

Set the following verses to your own **original** music. You can write a piece for voice (or voices) and accompanying instrument (or instruments). **Or** you can compose an instrumental piece that illustrates the **mood** of the verses. You can choose your own instruments, but make sure you name the instrument or instruments on the score.

See Core Book page 204 for some helpful hints. You will need your own manuscript book or pad.

1 A Tiger in the Zoo

He stalks in his vivid stripes
The few steps of his cage,
On pads of velvet quiet,
In his quiet rage.   Leslie Norris

2 Human Family

I note the obvious differences
Between each sort and type,
But we are more alike, my friends,
Than we are unalike.   Maya Angelou

3 A Christmas Childhood

My father played the melodeon
Outside at our gate;
There were stars in the morning east
And they danced to his music.   Patrick Kavanagh

4 My Luve is like a Red, Red Rose

O, my luve's like a red, red rose,
That's newly sprung in June:
O, my luve's like the melodie,
That's sweetly play'd in tune.   Robert Burns

5 The Listeners

"Is there anybody there?" said the Traveller,
Knocking on the moonlit door;
And his horse in the silence champed the grasses
Of the forest's ferny floor.   Walter De La Mare

6 The Lake Isle of Innisfree

I will arise and go now, for always night and day
I hear lake water lapping with low sounds by the
    shore;
While I stand on the roadway, or on the
    pavements grey,
I hear it in the deep heart's core.   W.B. Yeats

7 Na Coisithe

I gcoim na hoíche cloisim iad,
Na coisithe ar siúl;
Airím iad, ní fheicim iad,
Ní fios cá mbíonn a gcuaird.   Liam S. Gógáin

8 Le Linn ár nÓige

Mairg le linn ár n-óige
Sinn ag tnúth le bheith mór,
Gan foighid, ach ag aithris
Ar daoine fásta suas.   Máirtín Ó Direáin

Aural Skills: Practising Dictation

Exercises 1–20

The first set of exercises concentrates on rhythms. You will hear two-bar phrases played on the piano. As you listen, concentrate on the rhythms. Write down the rhythm of each two-bar phrase. Watch out for the ♩. ♪ rhythm, which features in exercises 15–20. The first one has been done for you.

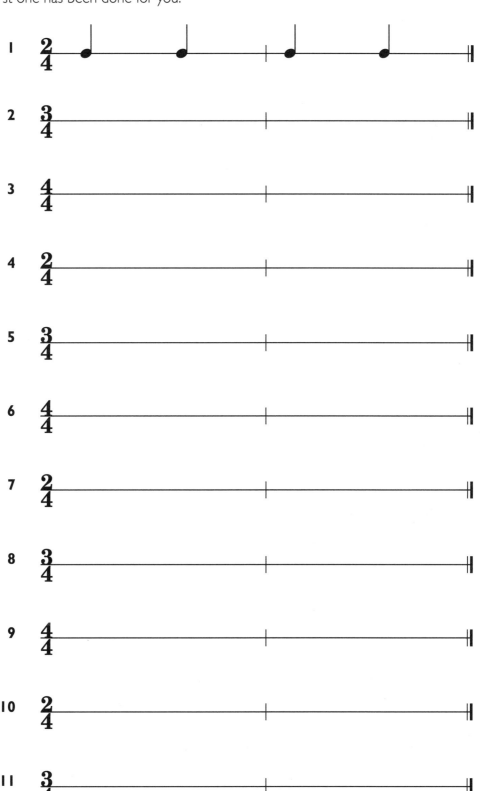

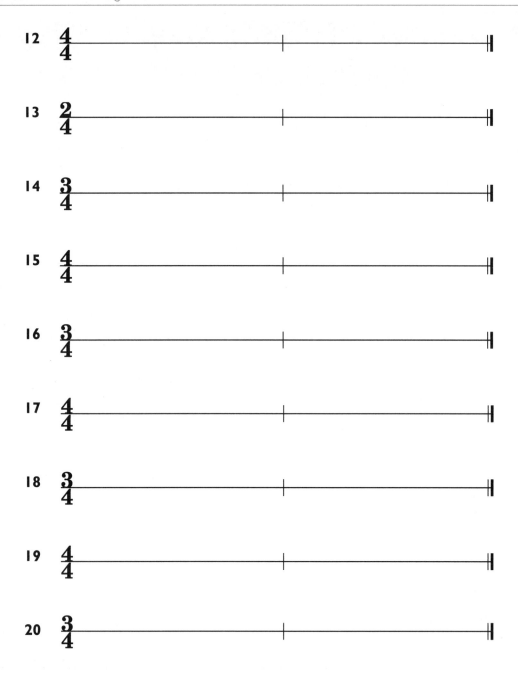

The rest of the exercises are **four-bar phrases**, and you must write down the rhythm *and* the melody. However, we will give you some help!

To write the melodies, you can choose between different methods. You can use:

1. staff notation

    or

2. tonic solfa

    or

3. a combination of stick notation (for the rhythm) and tonic solfa.

Exercise 21

Listen carefully to the following four-bar phrase.

The rhythm has been provided to help you.

Work out the missing solfa and write the melody on the stave. You will hear the keynote (doh) and tonic chord, then one bar of metronome leading into the melody.

doh = C

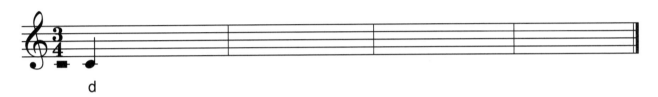

d

Exercises 22–25

Listen carefully to the these four-bar phrases. Work out the rhythm and the remaining melody notes. Bars 1 and 3 have been provided to help you, so you have to work out bars 2 and 4. You will hear the keynote (doh) and tonic chord, then one bar of metronome leading into the melody.

You can write bars 2 and 4 in staff notation **or** tonic solfa **or** using stick notation and solfa.

22 Track 43

staff notation (doh = G)

d

Tonic solfa

| d :– |m : s | d : m| s : m |

Stick notation with solfa letters

23 Track 44
Doh = D

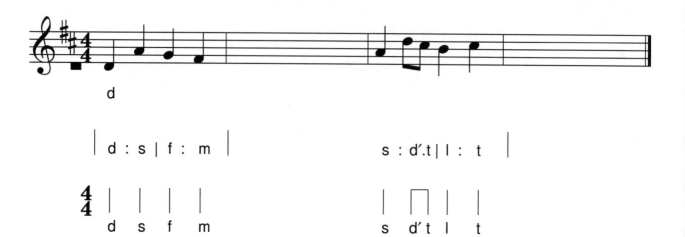

d

| d : s | f : m | | s : d'.t | l : t |

<pre>
4 | | | | | ⊓ | |
4 d   s   f   m   s d't l   t
</pre>

24 Track 45
Doh = B♭

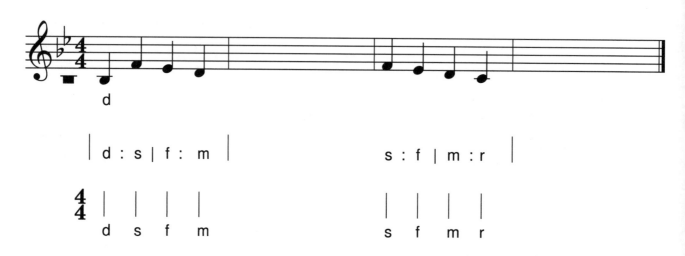

d

| d : s | f : m | | s : f | m : r |

<pre>
4 | | | | | | | |
4 d   s   f   m   s   f   m   r
</pre>

25 Track 46
Doh = C

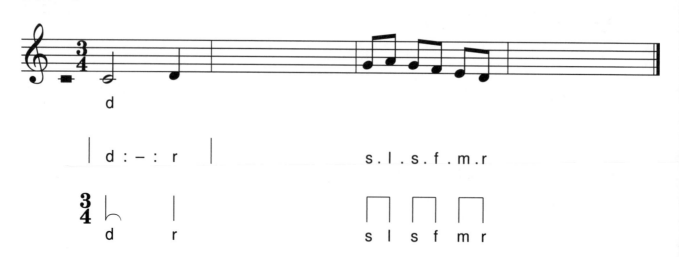

d

| d : – : r | | s . l . s . f . m . r |

<pre>
3 ⌐ | ⊓   ⊓   ⊓
4 d   r   s l s f m r
</pre>

Exercises 26–40

Listen carefully to the these four-bar phrases. Work out the rhythm and the remaining melody notes. Put in the barlines.

Try to practise these in exam conditions:

- Repeat each phrase FIVE times.
- The keynote (doh) and the tonic chord will be sounded before each playing.
- You will hear the pulse on the metronome before and during the first TWO playings ONLY.

26 Doh = F Tracks 47 (with metronome click) and 48 (without click)

27 Doh = D Tracks 49 (with metronome click) and 50 (without click)

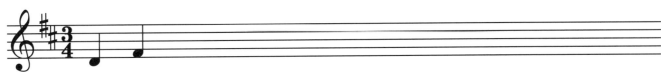

28 Doh = C Tracks 51 (with metronome click) and 52 (without click)

29 Doh = G Tracks 53 (with metronome click) and 54 (without click)

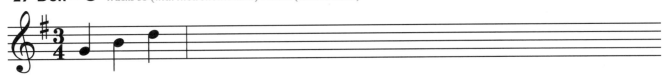

30 Doh = D Tracks 55 (with metronome click) and 56 (without click)

31 Doh = F Tracks 57 (with metronome click) and 58 (without click)

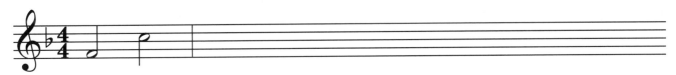

32 Doh = C Tracks 59 (with metronome click) and 60 (without click)

33 Doh = G Tracks 61 (with metronome click) and 62 (without click)

34 Doh = F Tracks 63 (with metronome click) and 64 (without click)

35 Doh = B♭ Tracks 65 (with metronome click) and 66 (without click)

36 Doh = D Tracks 67 (with metronome click) and 68 (without click)

37 Doh = G Tracks 69 (with metronome click) and 70 (without click)

38 Doh = F Tracks 71 (with metronome click) and 72 (without click)

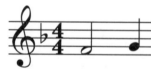

39 Doh = B♭ Tracks 73 (with metronome click) and 74 (without click)

40 Doh = F Tracks 75 (with metronome click) and 76 (without click)

14 | Performing Skills

My Performing Plan

Higher Level ☐ **or** Ordinary Level ☐

If Higher Level, one activity ☐ **or** two activities ☐

Voice ☐ **or** Instrument ☐

If instrument, which instrument? ☐

Sight-reading ☐ **or** Aural Memory Test ☐

Solo ☐ **or** Group ☐

Higher Level

If one activity:

Name of piece and composer

1 _____

2 _____

3 _____

4 _____

If two activities:

ACTIVITY 1: _____

Name of piece and composer

1 _____

2 _____

ACTIVITY 2: _____

Name of piece and composer

1 _____

2 _____

Ordinary Level — One activity only

Name of piece and composer

1 _____

2 _____

Practising

- Be consistent. Practise regularly and often!
- Work on weaker parts of the piece when you begin.
- Play slowly to improve and gradually build up to full tempo.
- Choose pieces, with your teacher's guidance, that are of the standard required but within your comfort zone to play well.
- If you are well prepared you will be confident.
- Create performance opportunities by playing for family and friends.
- Work on phrasing and breathing.
- Singers: clear diction is essential, clear words.
- Dynamics – getting louder and softer – and playing with expression are very important.
- Play pieces you enjoy!

Sight-reading or Aural Memory Tests

These are worth 20% of the 100 marks for performing, so prepare well.

Sight-reading should be a regular part of your instrumental practice routine.

- Scan through.
- Look carefully at places with a bit of a challenge.
- Note the key signature.
- Play at a manageable tempo, keeping the momentum going.

Aural memory rhythm tests are 4-bar melodies which the candidate claps back.

- The examiner plays the CD track twice.
- The candidate claps the rhythm pattern (first attempt).
- The examiner plays the test again, one more time.
- The candidate claps the rhythm pattern again (second attempt).
- The better attempt of the two is marked by the examiner.

Aural memory melody tests are conducted as above, except that the candidate sings back the melody instead of clapping the rhythm.

On the Exam Day

- Be in school early, and warm up vocally or on your instrument.
- Keep focused before your slot, and think carefully about tempo and expression.
- When you go into the exam, sign the roll where the examiner indicates.
- Set yourself up with a music stand, and check tuning if necessary.
- If you are nervous, remember to take good deep breaths.
- Begin confidently.
- Stay focused.
- Enjoy the performance. This will be communicated to the listener, the examiner.
- Take all the time you are allowed when looking at the sight reading.

15 | What I Need to Know for the Junior Certificate

You can complete the charts in this chapter as you progress through the course —especially in third year, when you need a clear overview of what you should revise during the last few weeks before the exam.

Performing skills are assessed separately (see Chapter 14), and marked out of 100.

Listening and **composing** skills are assessed in the examination, as described in this chapter, and marked out of 300. The tables below show the subjects you have to answer questions about in the exam, and the mark scheme:

Higher Level		
Question 1	Set songs	30 marks
Question 2	Set works	30 marks
Question 3	Irish music	40 marks
Question 4	Dictation	40 marks
Question 5	Chosen songs or works	40 marks
Question 6	Triads	20 marks
Question 7	Melody-writing	35 marks
Question 8	Chord progressions	45 marks
Question 9 (this question may be selected **instead of** questions 6, 7 and 8	Free composition	100 marks
Question 10	Chosen General Study	20 marks

Ordinary Level		
Question 1	Set songs	30 marks
Question 2	Set works	30 marks
Question 3	Irish music	40 marks
Question 4	Dictation	40 marks
Question 5	Chosen songs or works	40 marks
Question 6	Triads	40 marks
Question 7	Melody-writing	60 marks
Question 8	Chosen General Study	20 marks

Question 1: Set Songs

See the **Sounds Good!** Set A, B or C Booklet, as applicable to your year. Summarise here when the songs are well known and familiar.

Name of song		Category	
Composer and/or performer and/or country of origin		Time signature	Form
		Key	Tonality
Notable musical features			

2

Name of song	Category	
Composer and/or performer and/or country of origin	Time signature	Form
	Key	Tonality
Notable musical features		

3

Name of song	Category	
Composer and/or performer and/or country of origin	Time signature	Form
	Key	Tonality
Notable musical features		

4

Name of song	Category	
Composer and/or performer and/or country of origin	Time signature	Form
	Key	Tonality
Notable musical features		

5

Name of song	Category	
Composer and/or performer and/or country of origin	Time signature	Form
	Key	Tonality
Notable musical features		

6

Name of song		Category	
Composer and/or performer and/or country of origin	Time signature		Form
	Key		Tonality
Notable musical features			

7

Name of song		Category	
Composer and/or performer and/or country of origin	Time signature		Form
	Key		Tonality
Notable musical features			

8

Name of song		Category	
Composer and/or performer and/or country of origin	Time signature		Form
	Key		Tonality
Notable musical features			

Question 2: Set Works

See the **Sounds Good!** Set A, B or C Booklet, as applicable to your year. List your set works here:

	Composer	Title	Section(s)
1			
2			
3			

Question 3: Irish Music

Make sure you know about:

- Dances
- Instruments and performers
- Unique features of Irish music
- *Sean-nós* singing
- The harping tradition
- Organisations that promote and help preserve the Irish musical tradition
- Composers who use traditional Irish music in their compositions
- Fusions
- Collectors of Irish music

See Chapter 8 of the Core Book, and revise what you have done in Chapter 8 of the Workbook.

Question 4: Dictation

In the exam, you will be asked to listen to a 4-bar phrase, played on the piano, and to write down the pitches and rhythms, and add barlines.

Practise by doing similar exercises from the accompanying CD: see Chapter 13, pages 183–186. Clap the rhythms to become familiar with the typical length and rhythmic patterns used.

Question 5: Choice Songs and Works

These are covered in Core Book and Workbook Chapter 5 (Choice Works) and Chapter 7 (Choice Songs). Learn musical features. Compile your revision in Revision Song Boxes for Choice Songs.

Question 6: Triads

You need to know five keys. Write them in these boxes:

Check that you know the key signatures for these five keys. Write them here, in treble and bass clefs:

Triads, chords and keys are explained in Chapter 10, triads in Chapter 11a.

Question 7: Melody-writing

In this question you must choose between three options – A, B or C – see Core Book Chapter 12 and Workbook Chapter 12a for information about what these choices represent.

- Have you decided which question to do – A, B or C?
- Can you write out the scales in each of the five keys?
- Do you have a plan for your melody?
- What solfa note or degree of the scale should you end on?
- What planning should you do for the rhythm?
- What range of notes should you try to use in your melody?

Question 8: Chord Progressions (Higher Level only)

For this question, like question 7, you must choose between three options, A, B or C: writing cadences for keyboard or four-part voices, or backing chords for a song melody. See Core Book pages 183–189, and Workbook Chapter 11b.

Make sure you understand the different types of cadence, and can write them in different keys.

Question 9: Free Composition (Higher Level only)

This is an alternative to questions 6, 7 and 8 combined. It involves composing an accompanied song to a given text, or a short illustrative instrumental piece.

This option requires fluency in composing and notation, and should only be undertaken with your teacher's approval.

Question 10 (or question 8 at Ordinary Level): Chosen General Study

See Chapter 6 (Core Book and Workbook).

What is your Chosen General Study? _____

What category does it belong to? _____

Name two pieces of music from your Chosen General Study:

1 title _____

   composer or performer _____

2 title _____

   composer or performer _____

CD Credits

Acknowledgments

'Joy in the Morning' (MCPS), from the CD *The Time of Snow*, by permission of Exeter Festival Chorus; 'Abeeyo' from 'Voiceworks 1 CD' (P) Oxford University Press 2001. Used by permission. All Rights Reserved; 'The Lark in the Clear Air' courtesy of West Ocean Records and Neil Martin Music and Roberton Publications; 'Dona Nobis Pacem' courtesy of Sony Music Entertainment; 'Evening Prayer' courtesy of EMI Music and Boosey & Hawkes; 'The Briar And The Rose', words and music by Tom Waits. Copyright 1990 Jalma Music Incorporated, USA. Universal Music Publishing MGB Limited. All rights reserved. International copyright secured. Used by permission of Music Sales Limited; 'Siúil a Rún' courtesy of Acabella; 'The Hole in the Hedge/Seamus Cooley's Jig' courtesy of Compass Records and Bug Music; 'Lots of Drops of Brandy' courtesy of Sony Music Entertainment and Chrysalis Music Ltd. All Irish Music dance recognition tests and dictation exercises recorded by Sharon Hussey (fiddle and tin whistle) and Seamus Brett (piano).

While every care has been taken to trace and acknowledge copyright, the publishers tender their apologies for any accidental infringement where copyright has proved untraceable. They would be pleased to come to a suitable arrangement with the rightful owner in each case.

Glossary

Articulation:	how notes are played, for instance accented or smoothly
Cadence:	two chords that finish a phrase
Coda:	an end section
Dynamics:	how loud or soft
Homophonic:	melody with chordal accompaniment
Interval:	the distance from one note to another
Ledger lines:	lines drawn above or below the stave
Legato:	played smoothly
Monophonic:	single line of melody
Polyphonic:	blending independent melody lines
SATB:	Soprano Alto Tenor Bass
Solfa:	describing pitches using doh re mi fah soh lah ti doh
Staccato:	played in a short, detached way
Tempo:	how fast or slow
Triad:	chord with three notes